Universal Ethos

Universal Ethos

First Published 2013

Published in English

Copyright © Johan T Burgh

All Rights Reserved

Category : Ideology, Politics

ISBN-13 : 978-1483966328

ISBN-10 : 1483966321

www.universalethos.co.uk

Universal Ethos

By

Johan T Burgh

Contents

Chapter

Section 1 – Human Identity

1	The Concept of Spirit	13
2	Universal Entities	20
3	Faith and Ideology	25

Section 2 – The Personal

4	Personality Attributes	33
5	Criminal Justice system	39
6	Mental Health system	43
7	Deprivation and Healing	49

Section 3 – The Collective

8	Capitalism and Democracy	59
9	Cultures sparring for Supremacy	77
10	Faiths in conflict	87
11	Nations in conflict	95
12	The Islam imperative	103
13	Territorial and Ethnic Disputes	107

Section 4 – Economy and Ecology

14	Finance and Banking	115
15	Economy and Environment	122
16	Ecology and Agriculture	127

Section 5 – The Way Forward

17	Primary and Secondary Needs	139
18	Journey of life through the ages	142
19	Renewing our direction	146

Preface

If we consider the state of our human condition, our experience of life, our experience through life, our journey from birth, nay before birth, from our conception, through the different decades of life and unto old age, we realise that there is a great deal to uncover in the mystery and awesomeness of our human condition, and how we share it with each other from our parents, to family, to friends and to other people with whom we share our experience on the planet. It may be something that we sometimes take for granted as we plod through each day with our different areas of responsibility and growth, and yet it is sometimes worth taking account of the value in our human experience and that of others and what we contribute to each other's state of life by the way in which we engage in public and social activity.

This text takes a look at the nature of our human condition, from a view of consciousness, referred to by the term human spirit. It seeks to review the undeniable universal state of our common reality, individually and collectively, suggesting approaches to renew our common identity and responsibility to and for each other at a personal and public level.

While first of all taking a look at the fundamental nature of our human spirit, re-realising the unique characteristics that we all undeniably share in common, such as the beauty in the many qualities of the human person, our many comparable needs, and the dreams and aspirations which make us all happy, it then takes a searching look at the many bodies and fields of learning which presume to attend to and provide for our on-going human interchange and involvement with each other.

The culmination of the text seeks to review the colossal myriad of activity, organisations, ideologies, theocracies, drives and aims which litter our world activity and attempts to suggest modifications which we could make to better honour the true recognised nature of our human identity, our responsibility to and for each other. It suggests ways in which we might better meet our needs, further to the already many great advances in provision by our developed world, and how we might further fulfil our potential and attain our destiny, by care for each other coupled with responsible use and care for the resources of the planet.

It further addresses the ironically, thus far intractable, causes of ethnic and ideological strife, instead recognising and realising our common ethos, under economic, ecological and political statutes, across international and inter-ethnic borders, in line with these supposed days of globalisation.

The purpose is to provide a wide-ranging review, from the personal to the social and public arena which might be of equal interest by those with political, ecological, economic, international, faith and ideological interests, with particular suggestions for public, economic/ecological and international policy.

Its propositions, though seemingly radical, are designed to take account of the current, perhaps precarious, nature of our world demography, economy, ecology and state of ideology, suggesting an amenable way forward for all, to further improve the condition of life, our collective spirit and our world order, for the benefit of all the inhabitants of this earth.

Section 1

Human Identity

1

The Concept of Spirit

In this interesting world that we live in, over vast generations of history, the nature of our identity as human beings is the divine material which has tracked our passage through life, has made it, moulded it, determined it, realised it and sometimes frustrated it and confounded it, as we practise and realise the attributes of human drive, to survive, be happy and to work with each other, with which we have been born. Irrespective of whether we think of humankind as a spiritual entity, the fact appears to remain that there are universal attributes which are common to us all, which are the necessary driving force of our consciousness through life, from day one, as we venture to live together, work together, grow in self, achieve for the betterment of mankind, sometimes failing, to live in harmony with each other, and to attain happiness.

Spirit might be the name that we give to this driving force, attributes of which are common to us all, and which lead us to be in common with each other, to achieve together and to comfort each other, as we build each day, sometimes simply to get through the day, and in other places, to build ever more sophisticated systems of life in which we live. The existence of this spirit is the innate potential that each new person is born with and subsequently depends on the adequate nurturing of the personality by parenting and socialisation. I imagine that many people would surmise that these attributes exist also in animals. As we share this world with them, and it may be argued that we are also a form of animal physiologically, then it is fair that we may share many attributes of spirit with them.

The nurturing of the personality and spirit is an awesome and necessary feature of life. This document seeks to cover some attributes of spirit, as part of the persona, as they evolve and persist in the living being, based on the successful, or otherwise, completion of the nature-nurture alliance.

The assumptions here come from personal experience, observation, shared experiences with others, and instinct, one of the many awesome natural attributes of the gift of being alive.

The definition of spirituality here is based on that profound sense of peace, centeredness, focus, well-being, belonging, containment and communication within a medium of connectedness to the beauty which surrounds us, including other beings, nature, our sense of God and our drive for happiness for self and for those around us.

It is possible that in those in denial of such qualities, a sense of these attributes has been damaged to such an extent that they have consciously, perhaps temporarily, discounted the possibility of recapturing a confidence and persistence of such attributes, expectations and experiences in life.

I believe that this loss of optimism in our spiritual reality is contrary to the purpose of human life. That, I believe, is a fundamental and universal state, hence my use of the term Universal Spirit.

Other fields of study may define this as the state of the fully-developed personality. It is precisely under such a definition, that we, as a society and as members of the human race, appear to differ in our view-point of the nature and relevance of interchange between each other on the level of universal spirit. That is to say, some cultures appear to lean toward a perception of a society as being a collection of individuals, whose spirits should not be dependent on each other, whereas some other cultures view a societal group as being heavily involved in mutual support of each other, and therefore more largely inter-dependent.

I consider it to be important, therefore, that, as members of the human race, we can come to a common understanding of the level of interaction and inter-dependence that is proper and appropriate, so that we may attain a level of society, both at national and international levels, which is less ridden by conflict and non-constructive interchange.

It is timely to recognise that this broader concept of spirit is perhaps already catered for by religious guidance under the many Godly influences and faiths which we have had in our world throughout history, and as such the recognition of love and our many sympathetic values under such guidance as the Christian gospels, and other faiths also, is testament to our common spirit, the nature thereof, and to the ultimate destiny of our human existence and our divine destination. The fact is that if we were to practice seriously the values expounded by the gospels, every day and with rigorous self-examination, our divine purpose would be met. The reality is that much of what is asked of us in the gospels, is met in the present day by those who practice love in action at personal, social and governmental levels but also there are many instances of dissension, failure to find agreement, injustices and greed which can capitulate in all manner of conflict and yes even unto wars, which confound our best attempts at finding a world order which is conducive to all and in recognition of our universal identity. To this end, unfortunately and ironically it is often between the many different faiths practised in our world that gross conflict has arisen, giving rise to us needing to look more critically at the statutes and direction of our various faiths, so as to divine the true purpose of our faith.

Thereupon it may be said that it is a facet of our human institutions that religions, faiths or churches are the bodies which purpose to define, contain and direct our spirituality. As such they are a medium, which seek to remain true to the original and definitive statutes of human nature as a divine entity, with human responsibilities, and which are a source of comfort, reassurance and guidance to their multitude of members.

But sometimes, at the edges, some of our diverse faiths throughout the world can tend to expound elements of conservatism, radicalism, perhaps even superstition or subordination, sometimes representing everything that is best in spirituality, together with everything that can be retrograde. Sometimes these are by-products of the inherent need for an organisation to define its statutes and boundaries. It is an unfortunate irony that sometimes, while trying to create definitive statutes, boundaries and direction, there can be conflicting and precipitating events which can undermine and transform, perhaps deform, the integrity of the spirit, which render willing participants ineligible. For this reason, many religions need to be open to the prospect of re-moulding and re-realisation in order to transform deforming influences, and in order to avoid falling into the trap of rigorous and inflexible self-righteousness, while being closed to the reality of involuntary deformed experience of the individual.

Thereupon, where some religions, or churches, tend to expound some of the negative traits, these detrimental traits may, or may not be, integral to the teachings of that church, but may instead be malpractice by some of its members. To that end, they may be practising false spirituality, and may be in need of profound self-examination and re-realisation.

That said, it is also an important requirement that religions maintain a set of core principles, based on the optimum true and just best state of personal, family and divine experience.

Unfortunately it is precisely in the interpretation of what is the optimum true, just and best state of personal, family and divine experience, where different religions appear to have come to radical states of difference, giving rise, absurdly, to conflicts, wars and unspeakable horrors which must surely be in contravention of any reasonable interpretation of the human spirit. What a dilemma. It needs solved, surely !

Therefore as the human race, we are sometimes at such odds about what is best for our human spirit, both individually and collectively, that we have a great deal to examine, deduce, discover and realise in order to perfect our optimum state of well-being for each other.

The vital component - personal responsibility to resolve conflict

Thankfully it is also a gratifying reality that when even one individual seeks to examine their motives in the light of spiritual guidance, especially by self-examination and use of innate intuition, a change of direction can take place which demonstrates responsibility, humility, empathy, forgiveness and character, which can change the direction of personal, social or even inter-race disputes ! This might be the subtle key to the resolution of many, many sources of conflict, and in the language of our present days of globalisation, from the micro to the macro level. It cannot be understated how much this attitude of mind is fundamental to personal redemption, world peace and attaining the targets of the gospel before God.

It is the objective of the remainder of this text, to examine and explore the elements of our collective human spirit, as evolved from the past, is our current state and as it might and could evolve.

2

Universal Entities

Have you ever felt, encountering some of the many bodies of people which constitute our human race, be they Churches, Business conglomerates, Ethnic Entities etc, that life, as part of the human race, is just one big game, in which we are mostly all tumbling and churning, with the best possible outcome being that we have experience of the best that we can of the attributes of spirituality, as often as possible during our lives, and ultimately at the end of our lives, and by doing our best to avoid being affected by attitudes, influences or practices which challenge or conflict with our best possible spiritual experience and values.

Can this really be the best possible way for us, as human souls, to live through this life ? Or can we construct for ourselves a true recognition of spirituality, which meets the requirements of all members of the human race ?

In our world, evidenced mostly by the advanced practices in western society, we have and accept, without objecting, faculties of study, learning and ultimately authority, such as Law, Psychology, Religion, Business Practice, Medical Practice and ethics, which, whether we acknowledge it or not, dictate the statement of our spirit but ironically also the practice and restriction of it. It must also be said, and it is fair to say, that, as a people, over the centuries and millennia we do, and have striven, more successfully in some cultures than in others, to build on the absolute facets of these fields, with evolutions and modifications, in accordance with new understandings and attainments, as time goes by. However, these fields of study and authority can sometimes be fundamentally at odds with each other, and still remain as bed-fellows, because they do not have a common and recognised universal spirituality governing their statutes, with which to find ways of living and interacting which are fundamental to the characteristics and rights of the universal spirit of the individual.

There are many instances of violations of the universal spirit, by recognised bodies who are bed-fellows with each other in these misappropriations of human treatment. One example might be - in the world of work, corporate closures, depriving of their jobs, employees in large numbers, contrary to consideration of the effects on individuals and communities. Another example might be infringements by one ethnic body over another, at various levels of severity, because of assumed superiority. Yet another example might be categorising of personalities on the basis of invalidity, because of total misunderstanding of the individual's needs and rights by virtue of his/her universal spirit.

Such examples can cover very many violations, from infringement of a nation's borders, to misappropriation of their natural resources by large global conglomerates, to denial of basic human needs.

We can see many occurrences, in the course of human history, of such unlawful practices. But it is also fair to say, and a reality through the course of human history, that we have achieved a catalogue of human endeavour to bring into being, statutes which attempt to make rightful provision for and within the human race. Glaring examples of these are, typically, the idealism of socialism or communism, or the benign provision by the laws and statutes within the western philosophies, to provide for the rights of the individual, national sovereignty and humanitarian need. However, we can also start to list many features of imperfectness in each of these philosophies, in their fractured provision for the needs of people in society. Hence there resultantly seems to be much that still needs to be resolved. We also do not appear to have reached combined intellectual attainment or agreement on many vital, fundamental and implicative matters pertaining to the meaning of our lives as part of the human race. Looking on the bright side, perhaps we have achieved to a very large extent, full recognition of, respect for and provision for, most attributes of our human need and directions but perhaps it has been tacit in its achievement, rather than lauded and expounded ?

Products of universal appeal ?

Has it ever struck you, that products of global industry may say much more than we care to admit, about universal commonality, by the proliferation of products, of which Coca Cola, denims, McDonalds, Smartphone or iPad are only a few typical examples.

By this, I mean that it is broadly accepted, and evidenced by studying the purchase habits of people in the developed countries and developing countries alike, that assuming of such products is perhaps one of the key indicators of an urgent expressed need of peoples to express and feel belonging to the supposed ideal human union. This says as much about the universal common attributes of our taste-buds, and, in the case of the jeans, a need to be held firmly, naturally, and in a pleasing colour, in the lower half of our body, the combination of all of which, leave us feeling 'cool' and relaxed, ready for physical action and feeling as one with our fellow human-beings. If you think about it, it is much more than just a fashion, habit or conformance. It is an inherent statement of our common human attributes and needs. That said, it is not, of course, to the taste of every human being to find a unifying experience in such products, however it is a very strong indicator of the tendency within human nature to find common expressions of our basic satisfactions in a very innocent, inoffensive and pleasing way. As other people may choose not to expound such common entities, there are a wealth of ways in which people have always achieved their own dream of beauty in the world through alternative arts, customs and ways of living.

Is it not time, however, that we address the meeting of other areas of human commonality, where we have so far managed not to find common agreement, to the detriment of peoples, and individuals, and as we still continue to fail in so many ways, as witnessed by conflicts, wars and starvation in the vast majority of our world ?

3

Faith and Ideology

Over the course of the history of mankind on earth, part of our reckoning with our existence, our consciousness, concerns over death issues and our feelings that we have in common with other humankind, has given rise to serious consideration of humankind as an entity which is spiritually greater than simply our physical makeup. This has taken the form of consideration for the intrinsic nature of our feeling of wholesomeness, the mirroring of qualities and being of others, and a hierarchy of respect for those whom we might see as being more richly endowed in these qualities. This can only be described as the spirit of man. Combined with this appreciation of the natural spiritual and mental gifts with which we have undoubtedly been endowed, by virtue of the fact that we have inherited these awesome abilities through our evolution from the generations of man before us, man has also entertained the idea that our spirit derives from a greater and all-powerful spirit who represents all that is good in our universe and world. The name we give to this omnipotent and divine presence is often called God, sometimes irrespective of the cultural background from which we come, although different cultures may see this Deity in something of a different light. It is no surprise then that mankind's journey on this earth has engendered faiths, religions, ideologies purposing to define and direct our path through this life, so as to help us to realise what is best in our nature, personally and collectively, and perhaps to constantly measure ourselves against the ultimate divine entity that we call God. To this end, the teachings of wise and holy men and divine interventions have often served to continually direct and encompass us within safe statutes for our own well-being and for that of our neighbour, and ultimately for total acceptance within the embrace of our directing deity. These spiritual bounds have peppered our myriad of societies all over our world, since the beginning of time, and for this reason, this text views the functioning of mankind through this prism of spiritual identity, whether some may see this quality as merely honourable qualities in man, or as parts of the journey toward the ultimate spiritual state to be attained.

Clergy as the adhesive in society.

Viewing society through the prism of spiritual identity and considering the building blocks of our collective spirit as being the many churches which populate our many societies, when we think of the life commitment and the role of the section of our community known as the clergy, it is interesting that a recent reference to their role in was as the 'glue' of society. It is almost humorous to think that this is best word we can use to describe the chief contribution of the clergy to society. It is humorous to think that it is such a banal term and yet I cannot think of any term which describes it better. Inherent in the reference to 'glue', I believe, is the sense that society's structures and communities are sufficiently fractured as to need glue to hold them together. Inherent in it also, is the sense that this gluing effect is the matter, without which we would not have a common spirituality. Can you imagine what kind of societal community feeling we would have if we did not have this 'gluing' effect. But what is central to our concept of universal spirit is that we need to be connected with each other in an accountable way, sharing communal responsibility for each other broadly under guidelines of the statutes of our various faiths, under the role which religious clergy currently fulfil.

A purpose of faith

It may be timely to remember that for those of us who do believe in a spiritual destiny with a loving God, our religious scriptures teach us that, despite the difficulties and trials which we experience in our life, we have been promised recourse to a loving God, to whom we can turn with our difficulties, our needs and those of others, on a daily basis, where we can find succour, inspiration, relief and forgiveness. It is the will of God that we find renewal for our daily journey through life, being refreshed by a healing, comfort and renewed happiness which defies and renews our relations to each other on our path of love and growth throughout the world. It is for this reason that we often hunger for figureheads such as religious leaders, or inspired world leaders to speak words of compassion, wisdom and leadership so as to renew our energy and commitment to make this world a better place for all our brothers and sisters with whom we live together.

Humility, Faith, Compassion, Communion and Love

So are we agreed then the fundamental facet of our human nature is that we need each other, we mirror each other in a manner which may be defined as love; if we have an over-riding sense of well-being, goodness and belonging, then it is our natural disposition to wish others, and in fact all others, to also be part of that loving experience. That surely is the pre-eminent disposition of our universal destiny. It would only be selfishness, greed, pride or superiority which might tinker with this sense of universal direction. The purpose of our varied array of churches might have more comparable features as a place where people may practise self-examination under the divine statutes of their faith, strengthen resolve to live honourably always, express, experience and practise humility, forgiveness, compassion, love and joy as evidence of our unique divine origin, belonging and allegiance. To be involved in such religious exercises, without acknowledging the unique rights and needs of every human spirit, would be witnessing to double standards and a denial of the nature of our true universal origins. For those within a religious organisation to be at odds with one another, is a telling sign of incomplete acceptance of our universal needs, from whichever faction it comes.

It is pertinent that different churches within the same faith tradition can often be catastrophically at odds in such a way. There is much ground to be levelled. To expound the validity of one church over another, is an admission of failure of common recognition of our universal needs.

What confounds the success of our society for all its members ?

It is probable that for those who think about issues of the improvement of society, one sometimes stumbles when we try to understand the reasons for so much crime, interpersonal offence, loneliness and personal agonies. But have we discovered the reasons and the solutions as yet ? Obviously not, judging by the cases brought to court or driven to illness, with a multitude of causes – and that is only those which have not resolved by murder, suicide or personal disintegration ! There is much still to be understood, applied and realised so as to take account of all our neighbours.

Section 2

The Personal

4

Personality attributes

The individual spirit

Let us be clear about from where human spirit evolves. Thankfully it is inherent in our human makeup, and an awesome reality it is. The beauty of the human spirit is named in the gospels, when we are reminded that we 'are made in the image and likeness of God'. Those who are religious understand this reality. Those who are not might see it differently, however no-one would deny that it is Love that is the beautiful and natural medium through which we share and communicate our spirit to each other. For those who are religious, how could it be said more succinctly than that 'God is Love', and the example that we are set in the gospels is the Love that we must be aspiring to fulfil in our 'Love of God' and Love of other. It is of importance that we recognise the attributes in the human personality which constitute the qualities in our spirit.

We must recognise that it is the varied positive and negative attributes in the human personality which dictate our deference for or against each other, and which can make or mar our collective universal spirit.

It is the field of learning of psychology which clearly defines attributes of personality which can make or mar the quality of our spirit. In the evolution of personality in the first months and years of every child's life, one model of psychology details for us such concepts as the child, adult and parent parts of the human personality. Subsequent to this concept, and what is important in this field of study, is the concept of the good and defective traits of child, adult and parent. These traits are direct consequences of appropriate or inappropriate handling of the developing child's feelings and the resultant traits learned by the child as a result. A typical example of this might me, where the evolving child has not yet had all its personal development needs met, and a new baby arrives in the family, whereby the parents are seen to devote more attention to the needs of the new arrival, thereby halting the meeting of the needs of the first child. Such a predicament may create jealousy in the older child, which can be demonstrated in all kinds of cruel behaviour toward the younger arrival. Unfortunately, if the parents do not recognise and take appropriate corrective measures to reassure the older child and continue to meet his/her needs fully, the older child, will, almost certainly, carry these traits right through life as an adult and probably as a parent, ironically, in a continued an never-ending attempt to punish whoever represents the 'pretender' to the meeting of his/her needs. This may come out in all manner of ways, for example bullying as a growing child and youth, being oppressive and patronising as a superior in the workplace, being manipulative or deceiving, being demanding or dependent in a personal relationship.

Many scenarios can be called to mind of similar, and often damaging and catastrophic examples of defective evolution of the child's personality, which can show itself in inter-personal or group situations. It is also, almost farcically, the case that often there may be more than one person in a group, each with defective parts to the personality, each vying with each other and within the group, in order to have their needs met, or their position of limited security upheld, and also to trivialise, demonise or reject the other's need. Sound familiar – in the family, in the workplace, in politics, in inter-ethnic strife, in wars ?

Therefore is it not time that we recognise the constituent components of collective spirit, so as to take appropriate and adequate account of the rights and needs of each individual, thereby enhancing and healing the spirit, individually and collectively ?

What we wish to draw from this interpretation of the human spirit, is the profound and definitive statement that the human personality both needs and deserves to be healed, for the good, and by virtue of the rights, of the individual and society. Anything else means that we fail as a society, and that is not acceptable. What does come out of this analysis is the need and right for the individual to be healed together with the duty on the individual to recognise the need for and engage in that healing.

This applies in family, work, public, national and international bodies, and the same rule might apply across all these borders.

The Balance of Physical Life and Spiritual Well-Being

Good parenting

Nurturing of the young personality is fundamental to maintaining values of a good universal spirit. Such attitudes would include total respect for the human condition, provision of all-inclusive affection to ensure the integrity of the experience of the 'child', daily experience which incorporates all-inclusive affection towards total wellbeing, practical exercises – play and learning for children, work and learning for adults, family dining together in a relaxed, communicative and loving way, open acceptance of the child's path to sexual awareness, a peaceful space periodically to strip the consciousness of practical concerns, and spend time in awe and in spiritual awareness of those beings and natural wonders in our world. Different religions, faiths/spiritualities may experience these spiritual values in different ways – the central attribute is one of awe, respect, love and union for whatever is the object of our spiritual belief, be it God or self, or every form of life.

We also recognise that there are many other instances and occasions in the course of human development, through infancy, childhood, adolescence and young adulthood, where failure to love properly for many reasons from inadequacies, mistakes, to circumstances and family break-ups, can render emotional and psychological injuries and scars, which can affect the well-being of the growing individual for many years to come. It is also a very sad reality that many who may have impaired experiences in growing-up, can turn to many kinds of addictions like alcohol and drugs, which can mar their lives. We need only look at the statistics for drug use and addiction in vast swathes of the developed and developing worlds alike. Wealth is no barrier to these tragic realities and much needs to be done to repair the causes.

If, in society, individuals have been failed in the above, then it is the responsibility of others in society, who have received such a functional upbringing, to bring to those in need, the conditions they need to encourage repair for the flaws in their experience. This can happen informally, or via statutory bodies, as it does currently in developed societies.

In reality this is how the better part of our society works, despite the fact that it is not always named as such – the fact that we have statutory bodies assigned to perform these functions, all-be-it that they may be inadequately resourced by government, and that it is taken for granted that voluntary bodies provide much of this vital need, with little recognition form the powers that be. What conflicts with total success on this front, is that all of us have not acknowledged, or agreed on the fundamental principles. It seems to be that it is our responsibility to ensure that all people abide by the fundamental principles, and undertake to live by them, in open agreement in society.

5

Criminal Justice System

It might be said that the broad causes for crime in our society fall into two categories. The first is as reaction to perceived inequalities in society to the disgust of members of our society who suffer, and deviate, for want of that accommodation. The next is perhaps personal grief as a result of negative experience in ones' lives. This may be as a result of inadequate meeting of unique personal and emotional needs within the family (or institution) in which one have been brought up and may be compounded by substance or alcohol abuse.

These are widely understood to be the precipitating causes of all manner of crime and anti-social behaviour, from violence to mental illness to inter-personal enmity to drug abuse and related crime.

I do not include in this surmise, wilful crimes, which are effected purely for personal economic gain, assumption of power of one over another, wilful ignoring of rightful ownership or for pleasure in inflicting pain. I believe that the primary fact which needs to be established in case of any crime, is whether it is for wilfully selfish, greedy, dominant or violent reasons, with unequal consideration for the rights of the victim, and also that the act is premeditated.

For the converse, where the offence is due to personal grief, then it is imperative that a different kind of treatment be embarked upon, which seeks to truly understand the causes of the feelings behind the offence and find agreement with the offended party on that basis.

It is possible that the subject relating to proposed legislation re 'compulsory orders', referenced elsewhere in this text, comes into this category, and that incorrect implementation of this ruling may be subject to gross violations of individual's human needs and rights. It is failure in recognising the needs and rights of the individual in the first place, which has given rise to the dilemma, and only a fool could assume that two wrongs make a right. I will work on the assumption that it is not fools who are governing our people !

By reason of Personal dilemma or wilful delinquency

In order to effect statutes which would reflect these changes in our perspective on crime and anti-social behaviour, I believe that it is imperative that judgement imposed on an individual must finally be made on the basis of whether the individual's behaviour is for reasons of 'personal grief' or 'wilful delinquency'. I believe that the terms of 'guilty'/'non guilty' should be qualified, without exception, as 'personally aggrieved'/'wilfully delinquent'. In some cases, there may be a combination of both criteria. If that is the case, then the aspect of 'personal grievance' must first of all be established. If this is the over-riding factor and the individual has been obstructed in rightful resolution of that 'personal grief' with the parties involved, then the individual must be given the right of 'provision of necessary assistance in resolving the root causes of the aggravation in agreement with the parties involved'. If the primary cause of the offence is truly 'wilfully delinquent' then a conventional sentence is in order.

In addition, I believe that the judicial system could change whereby, individuals, whose crimes fit into the category of 'wilfully delinquent', could be given initially the option for treatment under the category of 'irresponsible behaviour which can be unlearned', prior to the consideration of mandatory detainment/ punishment. Whether residential detainment is necessary in all categories of offence, would also depend on whether the individual can be trusted not to offend in public again, subject to the direction of the administering departments, and whether the necessary care/treatment can be achieved to satisfactory completion for the parties concerned.

I believe that it is implementation of these new statutes which are vitally required in order to minimise the extent of compulsory incarceration, as it exists in, not least, the UK, to the present day. It is also necessary so as to ensure that the offender receives and achieves a modification in life-style so as to prevent repeat offending.

I believe that our current system, yes in this 21st century, is draconian, inadequate and boorish, with the losers being the offending individuals as well as the victims of crime, in wastage of life, and also the whole of society, as beholders of such an inadequate regime. The purpose to be attained must surely be to facilitate every human being, not least the offender, to attain the human experience which they rightly deserve by virtue of being human.

Without such an all-inclusive review of the judicial system, we fail miserably to recognise the abundance of personally grief-ridden people, who are thrown together with wilful criminals. The system is failing innocent individuals in a, possibly, criminal manner. Can a legal system possibly continue to preside over such abomination ?

In the new system, on the advent of a new crime/case, the magistrate/judge must initially make an interim judgment on the probable precipitating reasons for the offence committed ie. 'personal grief' or 'wilful delinquency'. This decision would be based on all of the following - the case put by the supporting legal representatives, the strict criteria/guidelines laid down in law for this purpose, the severity of the crime committed and the spontaneity, or otherwise, of the crime committed.

The case of bail etc would continue to apply on the same grounds as currently.

6

Mental Health System

It is from the afore-mentioned look at the precipitating causes for an offence, that we gather a deeper understanding of a state of personal grief as a cause of, not only crime, but also personal distress and mental illness.

It is the subject of mental distress/illness which now also needs reviewing. There are several probable causes of mental distress/illness, some of which are the following :- heredity, unbearable personal life-experience, traumatic experience (involuntary or otherwise), enduring deprivation of personal rights and needs by other(s), misuse of illegal substances or drugs, as a result of physical brain-damage. Mental distress/illness is arguably the most awful state that a human being can ever have to endure.

It is fundamentally an excessively severe assault on the very spirit of the human being and, not least for this reason, it should be in receipt of the utmost care and attention in resolving by us as a society, for the sake of the individual and society.

I believe that there must be a broadening of the scope of understanding and care for individuals who are in the grip of mental illness/distress, in conjunction with the changes to the legal system purposed earlier.

This approach should undertake an initial assessment by the professional as to the truly probable cause of the episode, again under strict guidelines and taking into consideration the precipitating circumstances of the episode.

This is so fundamental that it cannot be emphasised strongly enough. The reason for this is largely because of the right of the individual. If a human being is experiencing some of the most awful and hellish things possible, then it would be a severe violation of that person's needs, to fail to establish the actual true causes of the condition, as a person cannot contend with a situation which he/she cannot understand, and certainly not if it is misconstrued by a supposed authority on the matter. It is only by understanding the true cause, that the individual can be enabled and facilitated in effecting recovery from the damage.

One of the criteria which must change in the care of individuals with mental distress, is the necessity to have full conference with the individual on the causes of the condition, so that the medical practitioner, the individual and probably agreed family/friends are in agreement on the true causes and the care package required for effective resolution.

Horrendous violations of the individual's rights might be currently facilitated by the inadequacy of legislation protecting the rights of the individual in this field and by acceptance of the medical authority's account of the nature and cause of the mental distress whether rightly or wrongly. It is also a horrendous fact, that, in the case of the cause being 'unbearable personal experience' the most likely cause is the inadequacy of relationships within the family of origin or perhaps unavoidable 'pre-natal' damage to one's experience.

These facts need to be established, by evidence of medical records of the individual's family, where possible. In the situation where the individual is acutely ill at ease because of the distress, techniques should be applied such as relaxation, gentle hypnotherapy, and comfortable surroundings in the company of the relevant qualified practitioner, so as to establish a genuine situation of trust and comfort for the individual. It is only under these circumstances that the individual is likely to come in touch with and communicate the most probable causes of the distress, or thereby find a curative solution.

This is also a vitally important exercise, so as to establish if there are un-healthy interactions in the family relationships which are in contravention of the individual's rights. In such an instance, the individual is actually a victim of an inter-personal injustice, and it will be a vital component of the solution, that any offending party is brought to understand the inadequacy of the relationship, so as to enable both parties to correct their life's experience. What is, and is not, acceptable inter-personal experience can be defined from all the knowledge that we have accumulated from generations of study of psychology, as to what is acceptable for the nurturing of a human personality.

The reason these vital changes to the statutes of mental health care is abundantly evidenced by such facts as the following. It is currently the case that there is no human rights legislation to protect the rights of the individual in domestic situations, other than between adult partners in the case of physical or mental abuse, and obvious physical abuse of children. Both of these are also largely ineffective, in many cases. If a patient suffering mental distress complains of emotional or mental distress caused by another family member, then the practitioner is limited in his/her ability to take action to have the abuse recognised and corrected, appears to have the right to adjudicate as to who to believe – the patient or the offending family member, whether rightly or wrongly and betrays his/her foremost oath to the 'best interests' of the patient by not getting to the bottom of the cause of the distress, and by imposing his mis-judgment of the cause, and by failing to communicate completely with his patient all that has been discussed by all parties.

It is an abomination of human rights that the practitioners, mostly in psychiatry, who purpose to legislate on the mental health of the individual, also preside over insanity, and treat all such individuals within the same institution. The mental state of the individual is largely in the hands of professionals who can ultimately, whether inadvertently or not, determine whether an individual goes insane, based on such criteria as the resources available, the money funded, or the commitment of expertise given. This, again, is potentially serious neglect by default. It presides over experience which is, arguably a fate worse than death, and is most certainly a failure of mankind to love and understand adequately.

Another related subject to this is the flawed distinctions between mental illness and personality disorders. This fracturing in the interpretation of the human mental/spiritual condition, is probably a condition of professional schism in the psychiatric and related disciplines!

These mental distress conditions must be viewed from the perspective of the individual's right to appropriate interpersonal experience. The distinction between mental illness and personality disorder as they are currently defined, is a gross misnomer, as these conditions are simply an indication of the way in which the individual has had to cope with almost unbearable experience, in the only way that he/she knows how, and in the absence of appropriate help and understanding from other individuals who should know better. It has even been suggested, in recent discussions regarding the proposed modifications to the Mental Health Act, that some individuals experiencing mental distress, but who are still having to be seen to cope with the pressures of life, misunderstood and unaided, can be defined as bad. The relevant authorities would need to do a lot of rapid learning and understanding so as to avoid being classed themselves as primitively ignorant, seriously negligent, in addition to draconian, on such vital issues of an individual's human rights and needs, and they had best act quickly to correct their stance.

7

Deprivation – effects on spirit

Attributes for adequate nurturing and effects of its absence

What might it be like to recall your earliest memory as being disconnected, and alone in a bleak, dark and empty place, in time and space, which has no horizon of light, hope and warmth and no seeming means to get to such a place, and where the only sounds are brash uncomforting detached noises which carry no conveyance of comfort ?

Might it seem that this experience called 'life', is a non-existent non-event, in an empty place, with no alternative, no prospect of an end to it, in the near or distant future ?

Such is the state of infant depression, a very real, damaging and enduring experience, or lack of it, which does not augur well for the future of the child, or for those who, in the face of it, fail to recognise and provide repair for it.

Could this be a myth, a mis-conception, and illusion ?– sadly not. And to fail to respond to such need could be a severe failing in the function of the human race.

Do you care, do you think it matters, do you think you could participate in the repair process for such a portion of the human condition ?

Can you ask yourself what was your earliest memory ? Was it productive, would you hope and expect that all other human beings might have similar early experiences of life, or would you not wish it on anyone, or is it somewhere in between ? If it is the 1st then you are very lucky, if it is the 2nd or even the 3rd, then you deserve to be helped. Do you want to be part of a recovery process for the whole of the human spirit ? It is possible. Let us explore the possibilities and the consequences if we do not.

The attributes of a Godly cradling.

Connectedness, feeling contained, in space and time, eye-to-eye communication and self-expression which is wholly satisfying, affectional accessibility, safe and satisfying abstraction, recognition of self and other as complete and whole, freedom to express feelings to the point of resolution, peace and inoffensiveness. Such things are the stuff that Love is made of, and the normal person.

The effects of a less godly cradling.

However, cracks in the 'cradling' experience can create inadequacies in these experiences, and prolonged or severe deprivation in these areas, can create a person who is acutely unfulfilled in any of these areas – eye-to-eye contact, thought disorder/disarray, affectional incompleteness, unmanageable/ unbearable feelings/ emotions, gross feelings of insecurity, impairment in creating Love in friendships and relationships.

The necessary medium and conditions for and a safe cradling

We are all conscious of the very primary need of sucking, giving oral pleasure and comfort, and the foundation that feeding, in continued life, is a satisfying, comforting and harmony-inducing experience.

What seems to be given a more woolly reception, is the attendant primary need to be held and contained safely, and comfortingly. This is the necessary foundation of a feeling of containment and safety, in an infinitely big and unexplained universe.

It is all very well to assume that every child is automatically balanced, secure and contained, however if the necessary attributes of oral and affectional comfort are not maintained, the results can be catastrophic to the evolving child. It could be a big mistake to fail to recognise, and facilitate the provision of, an adequately nurturing package for the developing child, and, unfortunately, if the needs have not been adequately met in infancy, the needs do not go away. They still remain to be met during the rest of life, hence it is the response of the wise person, to facilitate the meeting of these needs, without judgement, and with affirmed confidence that meeting the needs, will resolve the distress/catastrophy. It serves no useful purpose for any of us to be unwise on these issues, or to deny their meeting.

It is a sad fact that Western Anglo/Saxon culture does recognise the validity of eg. Smoking as an oral re-assurance of comfort, but is anathoma to the free giving of affection or simply touch, which is an equally, if not more vital contributing attribute of the secure and balanced human being.

Alas our society bears the scars of this incomplete provision, as may be evidenced by such events as the massive and tangible grief demonstrated at the time of the death of Princess Diana in the late 1990s. It cannot be denied that the very deep feelings which were touched by the passing of someone who reached out in body, empathy and sincerity, surpasses anything known to western society and beyond, for decades and perhaps centuries. It was not that Princess Diana, of herself, was a complete expression of emotional well-being, far from it, but that from her sensitivity and great need, she genuinely reached to those who were also in great need ie. to give support and comfort in the face of unendurable discomfort and distress. This speaks volumes, which we could ignore at our peril.

Healing for Deprivation

The following surmises on the catastrophic effects of prolonged/acute deprivation to a developing child, where the nurturing/relationship needs have not been addressed.

What would happen to a little child, if its mother/carer does not give it the all-inclusive care and nurturing that it requires, as an infant.

If the child is left depleted in sucking, being held secure, having re-assuring sounds, re-assuring eye-to-eye contact, acknowledgement of expression of feelings, or depression on the part of the carer, what would the effects be ?

Would the child fail to gain confidence in the act which is not fostered? Might the child develop into a mood of doubt, lack of joy, lack of confidence, sporadicness of self-expression ?

What would the child be doing if it falls into any of these states ? Would he/she make self-expression, only when it can muster the energy and direction, into open space, or possibly to another responsive carer, go around in circles of inadequate experience, misbehave, or behave dysfunctionally, be seen to be in a state of sadness/ disillusion/ vacantness/ withdrawal or be so vacant/disillusioned as to try to hide showing this, as it does not invite love, thereby living with a mask to the real state of psychological health.

What should the responsible carer do, on finding a child in this situation ? Should the carer agree that the child deserves not to have to feel this way, should be understood for the reasons giving rise to this condition, should have provision made to provide a carer who will reverse the circumstances which gave rise to the situation, either by re-training the original carer/parent, or bringing the child into a carer situation which genuinely provides the child with the unconditional one-to-one reassurance which re-activates the child's ability to exist in a positive space, and to be able to 'over-write' the experience of the error condition. Should it not certainly be agreed that the child should no longer be subjected to the precipitating causes ?

Does it make any sense to allow the 'cracks' in the child's experience to stay open/ unacknowledged/ unattended – what would the outcome of that be ? Would anyone gain from that ?

If the situation does go unaddressed, then might the effects on the child's state be broken confidence in personal feelings, broken ability to make real friends or nervousness, demonstrated by smoking, dependence, or chronic shyness. What might be the implications for the child's mental health ? Might he/she verge on paranoia, reticence, unbearable anger/grief, embarrassment ? What do you think would be the level of effect on the child, depending on the level of the deprivation ? Would there would be a 'floor' to the feelings or might the level of distress be as ghastly in its feeling as the extent of the deprivation ? That is to say, if there was very extensive deprivation, could there be bottomless awfulness to the feelings of the child ? Might the child have feelings/experiences/state of being, which could incorporate 'monsters', desolation ie. Like feeling alone in outer space, feelings of not being a person – how bearable would that be, feelings of enormous distance from a state of well-being, ie a lot of ground to cover in order to get into a state of normal human comfort with another person, and no skills for getting there, and no hope of the situation improving, an unbearably long life ahead in this detached, desolate, lonely and miserable state, re-enforcement of rejection from each other individual met because of inadequate feelings to share ?

What would be the 'physical' feelings associated with this? Might they be excessive blushing, postural awkwardness, high levels of nervous agitation, not being comfortable or deeply relaxed in one's skin, inability to invite suitable stimulation from another, because of these symptoms, hence worsening the state of incompleteness ?

What might the intellectual/relational effects be ? Might they be incomplete abstraction and hence an impairment on the ability to communicate in a 3D and comfortable manner to another, impairment to the ability of the child to get peaceful and adequate satisfaction from completing tasks by itself/playing, working, musing alone.

Then what would be the ingredients of care which could reverse this frightful situation. Perhaps it would be touch, gentle and casual, as well as periodic and assured, acknowledgment of feelings expressed, and evoked, by the intelligence of the carer, for completeness-sake, regular and frequent encouragement to the child to obtain satisfaction by complete expression of feelings, including joy and boisterousness, so as to eliminate the boredom and isolation felt by not doing so, and so as to remain connected with others, total belief in the fact that the child must be supported all-the-way to the point of success, and not doubted, abandoned or neglected, paying attention to the psycho-physical expression of the child's state ie. Nervousness, tears, blushing/ embarrassment, and ultimately personal comfort and deep peace, and hopefully ultimately, clarity, until the process is complete.

And what would the implications be if this care is not given ? Perhaps broken connectedness for the individual, not being OK ie. Not feeling connected to a warm, loving and enclosing life, a supposed 'guilt' for not feeling OK, prolonged loneliness, boredom and sadness, time wasted in not being part of, and contributing to, a warm enclosed presence for everyone.

It must also be said here that this scenario could also apply to many in our world who have had developmental issues in the form of learning disabilities or any disability, and whose path of learning through life is rarely a straight one. The same care and attention are also required here as mandatory.

What is required is that there is a committed carer to see the process through. Might the child repair one-to-one damage on its own ? I don't think so.

Section 3

The Collective

8

Capitalism and Democracy

Bearing in mind that first penning of this book was in 2001, before the events of 9/11 and long before the huge world economic crash of 2008/9, in global socio-economic and political life, we are currently living through a period in human history where global capitalism has been top dog, since the end of the cold war. This is evidenced by such practices as global free-market economy in operation, presumption of Western moral high-ground on military superiority over eg. objecting Arabic/Muslim middle-eastern countries and global business organisations which function in countries which traditionally were not subscribing to capitalistic philosophy, for example China and Russia.

Capitalism

On the grounds that it has provided the incentives and the answers to many practical and growth problems over several generations, the economic functioning of capitalism and has won spontaneous allegiance from many peoples who have come under its influences, which proves its innate congeniality to many peoples. However, while it provides competition for excellence, we must remember that there are differing grades of capitalism, typified by, for example, the US/UK model, as opposed to the more tempered European model typified by that of the economies of Germany or France, or the even more successful examples of the Nordic countries, where a refined balance of economic growth, ecological awareness, and a much greater sense of economic equality for their citizens makes a society which has greater moral and material equilibrium, giving rise to greater happiness. The differences therein shine a light on aspects of capitalism which may not be conducive to human happiness or to ecological balance with the natural world. This chapter seeks to elucidate opposing aspects of the dominant economic model, with suggestions for how it might be transformed to facilitate a method which brings greater harmony, standard of living and well-being to many of the peoples of the world.

On the other hand, Democracy

It is one of the many interesting revelations of this interesting world that we live in, that the medium of democracy is a channel by which many peoples seek to live, which provides consent in harmony over the myriad of issues that pertain to our human lives from local administration to legal systems, to health care, from infrastructure planning to equality issues over everything from gender to faith allegiances, and from environmental issues to international policy. As such it is a most vital and life-enhancing medium and is not so much referred to by such a grandiose term as an ideology, more as a successful way of life, which represents harmonious agreement between many peoples with differing opinions.

As such, democracy is a vital component in mankind's drive to achieve harmonious living on our planet, but it is only one of the many arms and bodies of progress, which need to be interactive in our daily affairs, which colour the journeys of peoples through life from their cultural roots to contentment and accommodation with each other. It is an ideal medium for attaining agreement on many acceptable ways forward, but it is also complemented by the integrative and parallel activities of ethical business practice, medical ethics, legal practice, equality assurance and ecological implementation, to name a few of the activities which pertain to bringing about just, public practice.

Multiculturalism

An added and commendable attribute under the umbrella of democracy, must be the relative success of **multiculturalism** in the primary western democracies, typically US, UK and France. As this is not something which is easy to achieve, it is to their credit that these democracies have ardently supported successful merging and co-existence of people from all ethnic and religious backgrounds in their countries, with the proviso that these peoples absorb and abide by the open ways and statutes of their country of adoption. Thereby, gratifyingly, a great deal of success has been achieved in recent decades in breeding a new generation of offspring, very proud to be upstanding citizens of their adopting country, while mutually enhancing their nationality of adoption in every way. Perhaps the greatest grace of this is that those coming from other, perhaps more disordered societies, are eternally grateful for the wisdom, tolerance and tenacity of their adopting country in supporting such harmonious integration, while allowing others to still maintain their private religious and cultural identities. There may, of course, be exceptions to the individual experiences of peoples, where such acceptance and integration is not readily achieved, and that requires to be redressed, but this can indeed be a great model for those countries which wish to embrace this kind of integration of global identities, however it is not without its struggles, and it is also not necessarily the desire of all other countries to wish to accommodate in such a way, and if that is the case then so be it. The world is big enough to accommodate different levels and states of integration, and as such is all the more colourful for it. However the tenacity of countries where multiculturalism is facilitated, is indeed a very admirable, if tacit and subtle, expression of the unsaid universal ethos in action.

Democracy, therefore, is arguably the most desirable method, or ethos, which needs to be applied amongst groups of peoples. However there are international issues which it cannot easily solve. Take, for example, peoples of different ethnic origins sharing the same country, where segregation is normal. Without resolving inter-faith disputes, which may be a very intractable problem for much time to come, it may seem almost impossible to find a way in which even democracy can work to represent all of the people comfortably. In such instances, it may take a long time, a great deal of thoughtful head-scratching, a lot of dialogue which is properly guided, perhaps often with an open mind about the outcome, to move things forward to a point where each ethnic group can feel upholding of identity, common governance for the common good, to which all agree, and room for unaggressive expression of culture. There are many countries in this kind of state, not least examples such as Iraq, India or even Nigeria. In fact there are so many, that it presents a major challenge to our world in the present day, and surely needs a suitable plan for action, to find a peaceful, sustainable and fruitful way forward for all. Regarding national determination for a way forward regarding a country's borders, that is to say, if consideration was possible for certain parts of a country to become an independent country, because of ethnic dividing lines, then that may also be a suggestion that is on the table, perhaps for a longer-term plan and by virtue of local referenda. This would obviously have to be in a situation of no pressure, but instead brought about by gradual consensus of opinion over future time.

In the present day, it is very gratifying that we have the example of the Peace Process in N Ireland over the past decade, which is a shining example of how such accommodation can be achieved, through honest and careful brokerage by the parties involved. As this is the country in which I live, I have been touched, as each day goes past, by the process of initiation, honesty, discourse and accommodation which is being achieved, through careful understanding of the issues involved, not without dissent, but with ultimate recognition that through understanding and mutual need to find accommodation so as to live and function together, we can find a way which functions within the common law and allows for flourishing and respect of different cultural identities. Surely this is the living out of our universal ethos, where the two main attributes are (1) functioning under agreed common statutes and (2) recognising and allowing for cultural and ethnic expression. A key feature of such a process is that it takes time for trust to be built up between the parties, such that an amelioration can take place, and that honest brokerage is an essential reality which needs to be in effect for the attainment of such a noble goal. It is perhaps the greatest irony of our day, that what we would be trying to achieve is not defined as a goal, nor is there vocal language in place to effect this. Perhaps the nearest hint of vocalisation in this direction is the declaration from the US that it is now more dilatory about being the world's 'policeman'. Perhaps this is just a first tentative step in the direction of defining and achieving a unique and much desired universal ethos ?

So much now, then, for our noble aims. But first of all we will need to look at the present state that our world is in, with the diverse features of both capitalism and democracy working together.

Capitalism and Democracy

It is worth looking at the combined statutes under which we live our lives in a western democracy and it will be enlightening to distinguish between what are the attributes of Capitalism and which are the attributes of Democracy, as they can be subtly ignitable in conflict with each other, while bedding under the same roof. Many of the features are as follows - motivation to have, and be, the best in everything, and to make the most profit possible in so doing, freedom and opportunity for ALL to have the ability to succeed in this, fundamental provision for, and meeting of, human rights within agreed national and international standards and presumption of the correctness of expecting ALL of the world to subscribe to this belief system.

Of the above, the first is a concise statement of Capitalism, the next a statement of Democracy within the arena of Capitalism the next a main feature of Democracy and the latter may be a statement of the combined effectualness of Capitalism and Democracy. Hence it is easy to see how we can become enmeshed in an assumption that we are working under the umbrella of Democracy, when in fact we are exhibiting Capitalist traits, and one can be in contravention of the other, leaving individuals who are executing statutes of life under these headings, in conflict within themselves over the rightness or otherwise of the statutes they are propounding. It is a clever self-deceipt and form of social decline.

While looking at the combined attributes of capitalism and democracy, as they are often coincident, it is vitally important that we greatly acknowledge the multitude of contributions that democratic societies have already, and continue to make, to attain justice, fairness, equality, tolerance, freedom, mutual respect, compassionate behaviour and freedom from fear, for all those who are prepared to embrace democratic ways. Therefore it would be a serious misnomer to fail to acknowledge these vital contributions to our ideal universal ethos by democratic means, while trying to better the path of capitalism.

For this reason we must be very careful in our re-examination of western philosophy, in order to identify and eradicate the flaws in our life-practice which are in direct contravention of the wholeness of the human spirit.

The Seeds of the Capitalist philosophy.

It is my belief that the conscious emergence and proliferation of the more hard-nosed aspects of capitalism, is based on a submission, by its proponents, of the attributes of inter-personal strife, competition, the competent and the incompetent, winners and losers. Capitalism can breed on these traits in the human personality and these traits in inter-personal relations. To its credit, in the face of confusing or indecisive scenarios, the pragmatic approach of this philosophy, while making good use of a healthy instinct to compete for improved excellence, can provide growth, hope, aspiration for improvement and industriousness. It is critical that the negative traits be tempered by balancing positive traits.

If viewed in psychological terms, negative traits would be defined as attributes of the 'dysfunctional child' and the 'dysfunctional adult'. Capitalism is founded on the assumption that these dysfunctional traits are integral players in the social arena. It thereby could tend to abandon the prospect that human beings can develop, live and interact together, using the 'functional' traits of personality and inter-personal activity, and as such can be a misrepresentation of our true human nature and an dichotomy of the human spirit.

I believe that, what may be drawn from these dysfunctional traits, must only be, the healthy form of competition, where the more competent members of society are free to grow in their contribution to society in accordance with their ability and leadership qualities, and also the healthy form of competition which evokes the will and desire to constantly become better at what we are doing. Examples of where this functional kind of social growth has taken place successfully are, say, when large Japanese conglomerates have worked together on agreed programmes to develop technologically, complementing one another rather than 're-inventing the wheel' in parallel with each other. Another example is where we see large companies being interviewed regarding improvements that they could make in their business practices, and where the interviewed party can openly and honestly acknowledge the need for improvements and undertake to put them into effect. This traditionally would have been more typical of the American approach to business, and, regrettably, the converse was the case of British business culture. Gratifyingly, however the differences between the cultures is becoming less and less distinct.

It would be a mistake for us to assume that discussion or debate of this kind is trite or academic. When we look at the statistics for criminal activity, inter-personal violence, loneliness and dissatisfaction with the rat-race mentality within the countries which are the main exponents of western capitalism, namely US and UK, we should remember that this kind of human misery is not an acceptable state, and we would be partial to the negative traits of the capitalist regime ourselves, if we fail to do our part to transform this system.

Degradation of family values – a dilemma in countries in the grip of Western Capitalist philosophy.

Is it not true that the true exponents of western Capitalist philosophy put the philosophy ahead of family values? Is it not true that the prospect of having a life-long partner in marriage can be regarded with patronising scepticism – likewise the idea of having children, likewise the fashion of having unvetted sexual relations with anyone, including with any gender. The attributes of being seen to be right and successful in all aspects of life, and superior in every situation of doubt, appear to be supposedly acceptable traits.

My reason for rejecting Western Capitalist philosophy as a universal ethos, in its current form, is because its evolution has incorporated and encouraged typically the negative traits detailed above, and for that reason, is not eligible as a spiritual commonality which honours the true human and spiritual needs.

Negative traits of Capitalism

And now considering attributes of capitalism from which secularism has grown, one aspect of how capitalism falls down, is in that, inherent in its sometimes aggressive competitiveness, is the need for the participating individuals to have adequate intellect, desire and ability to achieve adequately on that scale, which may not be fair to many individuals.

Such objections as the anti-capitalist rallies seen in recent decades in the western world, are examples of masses of the population who do not feel that they have, or wish to share, these pre-requisites of being capitalist. As such, their perspective deserves to be understood. Perhaps we can all learn something from it. It is a little tragic, that, until now, since the growth of global capitalism, there has been no medium for valid reasoning, or expressing of objection or alternative to it. Is it not now high time that we get our thinking caps on? On a positive note, it is perhaps a very healthy reality that there are many people who choose to live a different life, not according to the narrative of western capitalism, whereby their lives revolve around a different beat, perhaps in harmony with nature, or the arts or alternative philosophies and it is a very important aspect of society that these alternative narratives can be clearly visible and clearly heard.

In addition to the primary attributes of western capitalism, we also need to consider some of its more 'parasitic' characteristics. I do not mean to be derogatory as such, merely trying to find the most appropriate term to describe 'characteristics which are part of the package', whether we like it or not.

Some of these characteristics might be disregard for the negative effects on those who do not make it on the capitalist ladder of achievement, irrespective of the source of their failure, naming of profit as the driving factor, rather than 'successful exchange' of commodities for all parties involved, be it financial or material, presumption of English as the primary communication medium, when the native English speaker does not make equal effort to learn the languages of other participating peoples, by excess freedom, acceptance/encouragement of immoral activities, including those which contribute to the breakdown of normal family life, values and relationship and inherent and subsequent breakdown in the rule of law to a personally and socially unacceptable level.

Tolerated side-effects of western Capitalist philosophy

Let us now look at the combined attributes and effects of such a philosophy namely, assumption of being correct in everything, presumption as the supposed master to other competing ways of life, hard-nosed business practice and ethical practice in all situations, material gain and profit by personal and corporate effort as a primary target, presumption that reason surpasses all feelings, assumption that reason, rather than empathy, repairs any problem, presumption that the understanding and taming of our environment and natural resources is the path to communal, social and global order, satisfaction and peace, and presumption that admission of incomplete understanding on any subject is a no-no. It is those attributes which begin with the term presumption which I believe to be the downfall of this philosophy as an eligible candidate for universal spirituality of the present or the future.

Globalisation

It is undeniable that we are living through an unprecedented time in mankind's history where the free-market economy has made possible a level of commonality across many countries at a business and style level, where national borders have become less obvious and similar standards in products and services are readily prevalent. It is certainly true that much has been gained and there is much comfort and convenience in, for example, processing of world-wide financial transactions. However the very apparent and precarious downside can be the type of serious economic and financial interdependence at the higher echelons of world financial activity, which has given rise to the catastrophic failures of international economic policy in the recent past. Also we may think that the globalisation that we know today is a new thing. This might be something of a materialistic illusion when we consider that in generations and centuries before us, there has been extensive trade on a global scale of desirable tradable commodities. Take examples such as silk, tea, spices. Transport of these desirables defied international and inter-continental boundaries at will. During these times also, the more common needs of the day were met by more local supply, and local cultures were rich in their own generic attributes. This is, I suggest, how it should be. Some attributes which globalisation has offered us is the more immediate abilities to address urgencies or crises across the globe, and by the immediacy contributed by sophisticated modern communication tools. Therefore, like many other features of our 'over-developed' world, there are certainly beneficial aspects of the achievements, but they perhaps need to be tempered by vital consideration of the more priceless qualities of our human existence and needs.

Untamed and uncontrolled industrial growth

A very critical issue is now arising in the consciousness of some quarters of the body politic, in recent years and decades, whereby we recognise that the nature of capitalism has been such an untamed and many-headed beast, subject to virtually no clearly-defined codes of practice or classical schools of determination, and often run by unqualified and avaricious individuals or groups, that it can be, by its very inception, an out-of-control and often dangerous adventure. That has been most clearly evidenced by the catastrophic world banking, financial and economic crises of the late noughties. Another way of defining this kind of reckless and untamed growth could be to compare it to that of an agitated **upward spiral**, with no particular destination other than incessant growth. If we consider the unprecedented technological and industrial revelations of the 60s and 70s, the races for achievement and the prolific, endemic burning of fossil fuels and resultant rampant pollution, it is no wonder that many where caught up as what can only be described as **octane-heads**, with perhaps an accordant addiction which lasts to this day ! We would be very blind and/or in denial, not to pronounce this aberration from the roof-tops, and to keep pronouncing it, until it is brought to a halt !

While a masterfulness in our approach to aspects of the many diverse attributes of our world is desirable, it is important that we approach many of the complex aspects of our natural world with awe and respect, as we are also custodians of these for the future.

When we look at some of the many natural disasters which occur worldwide such as tsunamis, earthquakes, floods, hurricanes, it is a timely reminder that we are not as all-knowing and all-powerful as we sometimes like to think, and that there is still a great need to humble ourselves to accept that there are forces greater than us, with which we need to be adaptable in our mentality, and around which we must more willingly undertake that we have more to learn. One pronounce feature of an attitude which might be attributed to the capitalist way of approaching life, is the in-build disposition to deny that one might be wrong in anything, that there is something more which we have to learn and understand. This could be classed as self-righteous, limiting pride. To have much understanding never precludes the fact that every individual should be constantly at the bottom of the ladder of a field of knowledge of which he/she does not have a fuller understanding. Only by such attitude can we be efficient in the intake of new understanding, acceptable to others who might challenge the completeness of our understanding, and ready enough to change our attitude or stance, when it is found to be in error. There is an enormous amount of intuition, opportunity for change and growth, opportunity for understanding amongst people and between peoples, that may be squandered to the enormous detriment of our own people and other nations, because of this kind of belligerent self-righteousness. Surely this must change.

Capitalism, Democracy and Christianity ?

In the words of one of the greatest ever writers and commentators on the condition of human life, Shakespeare, 'Ah there's the rub !' At this point in history, it is interesting that the current version of democracy and capitalism which has predominated over the past 200 years, exists primarily in the western world, and has evolved largely from the white western Christian roots. Of course there have been many great civilisations before throughout the course of history, not least in ancient China or the Middle East and the ancient peoples of South America. However the current state of evolution of our present world order in this day has grown largely from the cultures of Christian Europe, from Portugal, Spain, Netherlands to France and then Britain. Ultimately the combined learnings of these cultures has culminated in the administration of the USA and thus western civilisation generally.

However we must note that this civilisation is not just a product of Christianity on its own, or of capitalism or of democracy, or indeed even just of the white man, but of a combination of the aspects of these things, working in parallel, and sometimes at odds, which has culminated in western civilisation. Therefore it is not the fault or a product of Christianity, necessarily, that there may be flaws in the life or guidance of the west. **And this is very important,** any flaws which exude from western civilisation must be understand to be defined as **secularism.** If secularism is something which dissenting parties such as Islam object to then it is not correct to class Christianity as the offending party. Christianity is a faith and religion and is admirable and noble in its daily pursuit of guiding and caring for the spiritual aspect of man and for care of our fellow man, in a similar way to the unarguable religious fervour and commitment demonstrated by the many who practice under the faith of Islam. If the objection of radical Muslims is to the flagrant excesses of secularism, then it needs to be defined as such, and tackled according to from where the errors propagate, which may be an offence to the spiritual identity or dignity of man, in the public arena. Many in the developed world may be party to aspects of secularism, but it is grossly unfair for radical dissenters, from whichever source they come, to classify or blame all individuals in the west of flagrant or damaging secularism. On the contrary, and considering on balance all the contributions of current western civilisation to qualities of life in the world, to the cause of good, to compassion, tolerance and guidance in international behaviour and to environmental appreciation, then we **must** commend that

90% of the contribution of the west is good, benign and constructive. However with any dominant philosophy, it does no harm to have opposition voices, and in fact may be constructive, so that we may cause to temper and control any offensive or damaging growths in that philosophy. However the responsibility is on the dissenting radicalisms to curb their criticism or aggression towards that leading philosophy, and instead to work towards remoulding and working together with the forces of good for the furtherance of the desired universal ethos which will satisfy us all.

Therein lies the onus on dissenting radical Muslims at this time, to reflect on their dogged jihadist inclinations and to halt now in favour of working together with western nations as proponents, and sometimes often as opponents, in realising the way forward which honours and upholds the true spiritual nature and dignity of man.

9

Cultures sparring for Superiority

Anglophilia and Francophilia

The term Francophile does not mean to emphasise French culture over, for example, Italian culture, or German culture, or Indian culture, or Chinese culture, but instead to emphasise the nature of this culture which overlaps with many other cultures also, but whose collective combination of attributes, features and ethoses are embodied more by French culture than any other.

Self-reliance, accompanied by cohesive empathy, I believe, are the fundamental attributes of whichever ethos succeeds in becoming the universal spirit, as it is this, essentially, which guards us against unnecessary self-indulgence, defeatism or excuse/reason for inadequacy/failure.

This world does not need masters, only leaders. Its inhabitants do not need wealth, only enough. What it does need is the spiritual commonality of responsibility and inclusion.

Western philosophy as an ethos versus Francophilia.

For those of us who live under the Western philosophy, it may seldom be thought of in these terms, but it would be foolish not to recognise that it pertains to speaking for us in our public lives, as the voice of our own spirituality. This is why we must be careful not to let it be our 'religion'. A revealing statement is 'Money is our God'. This shows how the positive attributes of Capitalism can inadvertently lead to an unclean spirit, largely because of the absence of adequate ethical teaching on the philosophical/spiritual front. Another way of saying this may be that capitalist philosophy has the attribute of enlisting by attraction, but not by teaching.

Some of the positive attributes of Western philosophy might be that by participating in the main positive attributes, religious allegiance is unaffected and unjudged. Individuals may practice freely under whatever their religious banner, provided that they conform publicly with the main positive attributes of capitalist democracy. To this extent, Western philosophy allows for the assumption of a spiritual commonality.

Where it falls down, is in the negative side-effects, which defy the purpose of a spiritual commonality. To this extent, capitalism can be a soul-destroying medium, where the individual can feel separated from the main body of the people, for any number of reasons, such as inadequate life-experience, through no fault of one's own, and an over-emphasis on the responsibility of the individual to embrace the capitalist philosophy, without any option, and, what can arguably be the most insidiously damaging aspect of capitalism, the absence of an inclusive attitude on the part of those who already practice it, which might otherwise be classified as 'Love'.

Another aspect of the British character's contribution to national and international bearing is that it is a world leader in the no-nonsense approach to all aspects of life. This is admirable in that it sets the bar high for all others to attain, and has the added attribute of being unaffected and unwavering by being challenged, when it believes strongly in the leadership it gives. An unfortunate side-effect of this stance has been that other people throughout the world can tend to flock under the umbrella of this ultimate leader, expecting to get rich pickings, where instead they need to be inspired to attain similar high standards within their own nation. This, therefore, is one of the subtle and definitive differences between Anglophilia and Francophilia, where Francophilia, while setting very high standards in public behaviour, it maintains the aspect of attaining quality of life within one's own culture, thereby facilitating an honourable and organic path to excellence, accountability and happiness.

It is the take-it-or-leave-it attitude within the British/American philosophy, which renders it unsuitable as a universal spirituality, and where the Francophile philosophy is more complete, because it maintains the quality of empathy in its attitude and bearing to other individuals, thereby guaranteeing a cohesion which is both beautiful, inclusive and, at the same time, based on the very important attributes of compassion, together with self-reliance and responsibility.

It is a fact of human history that Capitalism is largely the child of British culture. In the same arena, are the socio-economic and political cultures of the remainder of Western Europe. These cultures might me described as cultured cousins of capitalism. As French culture was the pre-eminent universal culture, prior to British capitalism, we now understand broadly, the terms Francophile and Anglophile to be the class of person who leans to one ethos or the other.

Nature-taming pragmatism or nature-embracing disposition.

Perhaps the following would be examples of the consequences of these opposing traits - as a living example of nature-taming pragmatism, the existence and persistence of concrete jungles with hellish features, where human beings are supposed to build their lives. What they build instead are hellish graffiti-ridden passages, urine-ridden public areas, drug-cultures, unhappiness, isolation and desolation, and crimes of every conceivable and inconceivable type or as a living example of nature-embracing functionality, homesteads in almost all rural areas of continental Europe, where familial homes are not ripped apart in the name of sterile modernisation, where having a pile of logs for the open fire is one of the daily chores which become the inhabitants, where village inhabitants exchange the fruits of the garden and the wild vegetables of the fields, where mutual imbibing of a good locally-produced wine or cheese, together with freshly-cooked food from the local market are the natural conclusion of the days living and loving. There is no reason for anything man-made in our world to be aesthetically-unpleasing.

To assume that these qualities of life preclude efficient practice in the fields of daily work and practice would be inaccurate. I draw your attention to such technological attainments as the French Minitel system during the 1970's and 1980's. The Internet and WWW of today are something of a derivation of that Minitel innovation. I draw your attention also to the level and quality of medical care provision in continental Europe, in contrast to that in the UK/US to the present day. I personally come as frequently as possible to France to revitalise my optimism and confidence in the human condition, to help retain my sanity ! - and to feel at one with every breath, smell, bite, sup and sound ! My vision of the more flagrant aspects of aggressive capitalist drive evaporates without trace, and a ready smile comes to my lips, eyes and heart !

It is the typical characteristic in the French 'savoir vivre' of the primary recognition of the importance of daily harmony with nature, the fruits of the earth and gentilisme with our neighbour, which trumps the more throw-away characteristics of typically the more flagrant British/American way of life. It is also of vital importance to note the success of free-market economies such as those in Nordic Europe, which do not exemplify the financial and economic failures of 2007/10 in the same way as countries such as US/UK and those of southern Europe.

The stoic and the epicurian

Another model of polarised ethoses might be the stoical versus the epicurian approach to living. To state the middle-of-the-road attributes of each of these, the stoical approach is one where the individual lives life in a practical, unexcessive, and relatively cool manner. The epicurian approach, while working productively, also partakes with satisfaction, in the natural gifts of food and drink, is freely affectionate and playful, and open and receptive to others, including those not of a similar frame of mind, provided of course that none of these things are done to excess.

The negative attributes of the stoical approach may be unnecessarily restrictive. Typically they are a judgementalism towards others who participate more in the joys of life, and a limiting of personal participation in life, which is unnecessarily un-joyful and perhaps not the stuff that love is made of.

Many people who actively enjoy the good things in life, are reliving the joys of early experience in being nurtured and sharing in loving encounter with others. What is attractive about this approach to life, is that it facilitates and encourages others, not least those who perhaps did not experience the fullness of joy and love in their early experience of life, to re-experience and re-find that joy, love and incumbent confidence in life. We, and each of our fellow human beings, only have one life, and it serves little purpose to make it any worse than it can be. There can be much suffering as a result of natural disaster, without us limiting or imposing limitations on the extent of ours, and others, joy-filled experience of life. The only value that I can see in any poor-quality experience is to give us the enablement to empathise, and thereby support and facilitate others who have equally bad experiences, through no fault of their own, to a point of belonging, happiness, joy, participation and inclusion. The stoical traits of being judgemental and minimalist, may be both self-limiting and restrictive of others, but conversely may also fulfill an important role in tempering excesses and lack of control, and providing the necessary mettle to cope with situations of austerity.

Another example of polarised differences in ethoses could be the tendency in the capitalist west, for our young people to grow up with the traits of 'being cool', choosing fast food and TV dinners, popularly participating in the drug culture, frequent extreme drunkenness, frequent casual sex of any and varied types, the all too fashionable approach to distaining the possibility of getting married and/or having offspring, or in contrast the tendency in other parts of continental Europe to participate normally in family meals in a condition of happiness and inclusion, to drink moderately in company with family and friends, to have and love children, as growing adults to be demonstrably in touch with one's inner child.
It may be that it is in the failure of family to instil the attributes of inclusion, personal and sexual growth, safe

and bounded experimentation, and the inclusive rewards of responsibility, where the young people of our society turn to the seduction of western capitalist grime, such as deviant sexual relations, abuse and excess of drugs, aggressive one-up-manship, celluloid escape, fast food and rejection of the family unit as a plausible source of happiness.

What reward there would be for a societal system which truly supports inclusion, growth and safety within the traditional family unit, to the point of mature, experienced, caring and productive adults, who can in turn provide the same for their next generation and the one after that and so on for ever! Why not, I ask you ?

I recall my mother often quoting a lesson given to her and her piers by a wise teacher when at school – 'Don't follow the fashion, set the fashion !' In other words, don't be sheepish to the point of brain-washed irresponsibility, instead use and trust your intuition – you might just find that it is extremely wise, as we have ALL been given the gift, and you might just make more brothers than enemies, in this big wide world !

An added complication in western capitalist society of today is the masses of people from less privileged or less safe countries which it has assumed, who are blinded by the light of commercial freedoms, at the expense of recognising better qualities of life in alternative cultures.

To put the final point of evidence before you, the figures for violent crime, burglary etc in the countries which most expound the western capitalist way of life, namely UK, US Australia and perhaps South Africa, are damning indictments of the fatally inadequate effects of an abandonment of inclusive compassion in all their dealings.

A way of characterising the differences between the two philosophies might be the following. The Francophile approach, while exuding ultimate appreciation of the finer things in life, demands high standards in public and personal standards, while critically, assisting this with compassion and joy as vehicles of communication. The contrasting approach of Anglophilia focusses on optimising correctness of self for ultimate performance, only setting example to the other in this practice of excellence, and ultimately minimising emotional discourse and inter-dependence in achieving progress in public life. Where I think this approach tends to fail is that, while providing high standards in attainment and also a safety net for those who struggle to survive in this system, it is oblivious to and, perhaps giving tacit encouragement to, various kinds of moral decline and depravity in the form typically of alcohol abuse, sexual flagrance and materialistic excesses. This is a crucial distinction, and unfortunately, has become synonymous with British/American culture to the world. While the contributions of Britain and USA have been enormous to our present world order and living standards, it is fundamentally this tolerance of social depravity which, vitally, spearheads such current dissension among other cultures such as the Muslim nations. To this end, I think it is vital that the British/American world publicly acknowledge this fall in standards as undesirable to the wider world, with intent to clean up its act by acknowledging past failures and by putting in place structures to better relations between people, so as to better respect individual, personal and spiritual destiny. This cannot be understated as it is arguably the most clear and present danger to our spiritual destiny and the state of our world order at present, with the current discontent in such countries as the Arab nations and North Korea. It is also the case that in so many emerging and developing countries, even such giants as India and China, the example must be set, and the wheels put in place, for a better quality of attainment on moral and spiritual grounds. This is fundamental to a better universal ethos which can meet the spiritual needs of so many varying cultural traditions. Perhaps it would be necessary for Francophila and Anglophilia to agree where they can respect, complement and combine each other's contributions with on-going acknowledgement of failures, for the common good. Thereby we might venture to attain a future which more greatly respects our common spiritual and ecological needs, with stringent uprightness, more ultimate cohesion, mutual respect and attendant disposition of union.

10

Faiths in Conflict

Myriad of different Faiths

It is an unavoidable fact of the evolution of humankind through our history, that faiths in a divine entity or presence amongst us exist in many forms throughout the world. They have evolved in so many different ways, but primarily initiated by enlightened, holy men through the ages, often proclaimed as messengers from a divine or omnipotent spirit or even from God directly. Examples of such are the coming of Jesus Christ himself, giving birth to the Christian faiths. Another example is Mohammed, giving rise to the Islam faiths. As we have all become increasingly aware, even within these faiths there can be separate and slightly differing expressions of such faith, forming separate religions and practices. In the Christian faith, these may be the Catholic religion and the many Protestant religions. In the case of Islam, there are Sunni and Shia and many other sub-sects too. And these are only examples of 2 such faiths. There are also many other major spiritualities including Judaism, Hinduism and Buddhism all from differing origins. It is an indication of how fundamentally vital is the need for humankind to have a sense of spiritual identity, but also consequently, because this is a vital expression of our very existence, where we have come from, where we are going, to whom we belong, that each party's belief in the justification of their own faith may feel threatened by the statutes of other faiths. As evidenced by wars, strife and disagreements over the centuries, these are tensions and differences which need to be understood, accepted and if possible redressed, for the sake of all.

Differing Christian Religions

As with other faiths, Christianity is sub-divided into Catholic and Protestant religions, and there is complex history in how these different divisions came about, which are much too extensive to enumerate here. Bur perhaps it is useful to define some of the many attributes of the main religions so as to elucidate the kind of different ways in which we wish to express our spirituality.

Protestantism

As is indicated by the name, Protestantism arose as a religion to stand apart from the primary Christian religion since the time of Christ, Catholicism whose leader is the Pope in Rome, the successor of St Peter. It arose as an alternative to the Sacramental and symbolic practices of the Catholic church, and chose that expression of its spiritual beliefs be strictly made by a righteous way of living closely according to the word of the gospel. It might be said that Protestantism's view was that aspects of Catholic worship which appealed to the senses and symbolism, were in danger of diluting or detracting from the primary responsibility to live every moment strictly according to the word of the gospel, and by word of prayer. It is arguable as to whether that is an accurate understanding of the Sacramental aspects of the Catholic faith and especially of the centrality of the Eucharist as being a direct channel of grace from God above. Protestantism chose a more pragmatic approach to living and working, without the support of the sensory symbolic and Sacramental characteristics of the Catholic church. As such perhaps their concentration of focus on stringent living has led to the contributions that they have made to public life over the centuries and, particularly through the pre-eminence of Protestantism in the British establishment, although there are also other dissenting reasons for that. It has also been a major part of early settler activity in North America and in might be said, has contributed to the evolution of western capitalism and democracy as we have it today. Traits of the British and Protestant character are steadfastness, honourability, resistance to being swayed in opinion and perhaps a certain steely pragmatism. When we look at the message of Christ, the one command that He gives us is to love one another. It might be said that Protestantism's version of this could be called 'impersonal love', that is characterised by setting an example and expecting the other, by instinct and by teaching, to attain the same level of righteousness and thereby to be accepted into the body of the church, rather than by emphasis on compassion and sentiment. That setting of example, may be an important part in maintaining a high benchmark for public behaviour, but it also needs to be tempered by playing down the aspect of self-righteousness and by on-going self-examination.

Catholicism

On the other hand, Catholicism, while living according to the word of the Gospel, is also faithful to the practice of the Sacraments, given to us by Christ on Holy Thursday, and through which Christ has promised that He is present to us spiritually in a special way, through which we may have direct access to spiritually experience the grace of His love and compassion in our lives. In accordance with this message of Love, Catholicism tends to be more sentient in its expression of love and compassion to others in its practices to others throughout the world, especially to those who are weighed down by serious difficulties in life through no fault of their own, and as such believes that we are redeemed in Christ by our personal experience and giving of love to another, irrespective of any other attainments or condition in life.

As such, because of the differences in interpretation and emphasis of the different messages of the gospel, these religions can come to be at odds with each other, which throughout history has been the cause of strife and even wars. Perhaps it is the case that Protestantism thinks that it is more practical about showing love for fellow beings, by bringing about development and progress, according to righteous and steadfast principles throughout the world. That is an admirable aim. But perhaps our God recognises that our human condition and our experience on this earth are not perfect, will be subject to trials and difficulties, illness and death and that without any unnecessary sophistication, the main purpose of our life before God is to experience and show love, in whatever circumstances we find ourselves, no matter how dire those circumstances may be, so as to be truly eligible to be with Him in glory in the afterlife.

In summary it might be said that the Protestant way's emphasis is on being pragmatic with plain speaking and acting where the Catholic way, in addition to living and practising honestly, allows for open experience of joy, love and empathy to colour our daily lives. I believe that the best attributes of both religions need to complement each other to work together in an honourable and just way always to better and improve the state of life for our fellow man, as an expression of the love that we experience from our God in joy.

But it must be evident that, as western capitalism and democracy have been largely evolved from white, Christian origins, the negative attributes of current western capitalism such as the attributes of competition for the purpose of profit, together with having a very laissez-faire attitude towards tempering of personal or social corruption by excesses, wealth or greed, are perhaps primary reasons for conflict from alternate faiths throughout the world, not least from the Arabic nations and perhaps North Korea. It is these flaws which hamper the fundamental criterion of the universal spirit, which is recognition of the mutual and common spiritual identity and needs of peoples, by emotional communion, untiring support and motivation towards fulfilment, self-reliance, until communion amongst our peoples is achieved.

Procreation and marrying human with divine

Within the context of religious practice, sexuality has sometimes tended to be seen as being perhaps in contradiction with real spirituality. This is something that has to be unlearned so that a person may understand and feel his/her sexual instincts to be a joyful, incorporated, recognised and responsible constituent of life. There has sometimes been the tendency to see the image of God as being outside and beyond oneself, rather than recognising that it is by being truly ourselves in love and truly human that we realise ourselves as made truly in the image of God. It is by this means that we do God's will and by being steadfast in living in an honourable and honest way which sets definitive example for others.

In the nurturing of children, it is in realisation of the child's personality by complete holding of its feelings during the most vital and tender periods of its life, primarily at the beginning of its life, that we facilitate the realisation of goodness and love for the next generation. One need no longer measure one's depth of spirituality by the number of religious practices adhered to or by contrasting one's goodness to that of assumed infidels, but by the integrity of one's spirit and of that passed on to our children and to others. The concept of evil can be merely a cop-out for lack of true love shown, and can be undone by unflinching nurturing and example.

Celibacy

Within traditions which expound celibacy such as Catholicism and Buddhism, it could be important that celibacy might not be seen as an ideal state of love to be aspired to, but instead as a personal expression by a person who feels capable of having such a great love for his/her fellow human beings, and God, that they devote most of their emotional energies, and self-control, into actions of meditation, and true spiritual love and compassion, rather than towards inter-personal consummation and pro-creation. That said, considering the extent and abomination of child sexual abuse uncovered in recent decades even within supposedly religious communities, there must be great vigilance to ensure that sexual deviance is not allowed to hide under the umbrella of celibacy.

Other Spiritualities and Traditions

Considering all the other spiritualities and human ways of living throughout the rest of the globe, having spent most of my life in the west, I cannot comment greatly on the essence of so many other spiritualities, other than to give my interpretation, assumed from those that I have met, from many of these other ethnic and faith backgrounds.

To meet, and come to know, people from non-Christian religions, can be a humbling, even humiliating experience, to find that white-western-Christian ideology, has despite its supposedly Godly beginnings, in addition to many facets which have contributed greatly to our world development, also typified unattractive standards in moral depravity and flagrant excesses in life standards. It is these things, in addition to the presumption that the west is right in everything, that give such faiths as Islam the reason to fly in the face of the west with violent opposition and aggression in the bid to create a new world order. We must surely redress and acknowledge these issues if we wish to continue to find the way forward.

11

Nations in Conflict

Irish and British nations as an example

Having been brought up in the Irish and British traditions, and having lived and worked in SE England, I have found myself asking myself and then explaining some of the fundamental differences in life-style which have contributed to the comparison between our ways of life, in past generations.

The Irish tradition has not traditionally incorporated a class structure. People are people, some are more skilled, or are more effective leaders than others, and hence everyone is provided for and density of population in Ireland is significantly less than in mainland UK, therefore there is less pre-occupation with meeting non-vital needs. It is simply adequate to have primary needs met on a daily basis, secondary needs provided for, and to find simple and mutual contentment in these. Therefore there can be less stress and more laughter perhaps than in the average

British population. It is a common mis-conception that the Irish have too many off-spring, as the population figures for both countries defy this ie approx 5 million in Ireland, approx 70 million in UK. Another historical facet of differences between the Ireland and Britain is the fact that the people of Ireland had enormous resentment toward being coerced to deny their Catholic religion, in favour of Protestantism, and are perfectly justified in doing so.

As discussed earlier, each nation has had its own contributions which it has made to life and to civilisation, some great and some more subtle. In the case of the Britain's contributions, it has obviously been a world leader, along with other great nations before it, in the development and implementation of statutes for every aspect of order amongst peoples, and in the development of all manner of scientific innovation for the betterment of living standards and health for all people of the world. And yet the more humble contribution of the Irish might be defined as keeping closer to the more primary needs and instincts of our human nature – meeting our daily needs for food, drink and shelter and having a gentle and unconditional love for each other, while sharing with other nations especially those less well off, by charity, missionary activity and education. These qualities are arguably the only and more important qualities that we need, and as such the example of the Irish in the world has been warmly accepted by other nations with a message of love and simple happiness. To that extent, it is not necessary or desirable to compare the contributions of each nation with each other, but instead to recognise how they complement each other, and how each realises fullness of spirit in different ways.

It might be said that this is the very interesting outcome of what has been a situation of conflict between our respective nations, in realisation of the Peace process which has been and is taking place especially in N Ireland in the past decade. Perhaps this is a concise description of how peoples who have different views of what is the best way forward for peoples, can dissolve their differences, instead replacing them with mutual respect, honour for positive qualities, encouragement for achieving honourable standards, understanding the perspective of the other, forgiving and leaving behind wrongs done, towards the common good, and towards achieving what is best for us all.

In situations of conflict within and between countries, it is shown, by this great example of the peace which has been achieved between Ireland and Britain in N Ireland, that there are procedures which we can go through to take the steps to acknowledge where the other is coming from and to build a mutual understanding for an agreed way forward. Two things which are vital in achieving this are firstly, a firm and unshakeable resolve to attain right and honourable statutes, and secondly, an understanding at all levels of the differences and difficulties for which each party comes. It is possible to do this, and to get up each day, renewed again to continue to achieve this, and never to need to resort to violence or oppression in the pursuit of one's ideology.

Sometimes in the balance of ideologies in our world, it has been instructive to have ideologies which differ drastically with each other so as to hold each other to account. Sometimes these are necessary, healthy and instructive forces which can constrain the possibility of an ideology growing into a deforming or corrupt entity, which may fundamentally be at the core of the strife between radical Islam and excessive license in Capitalism

In the case of situations where peoples are at odds with each other's deviances or inadequacies, it is necessary for each party to examine their way of life or behaviour, to see if there are ways in which they live falls short of the standards expected for respect of self and respect of other, where behaviour deviates from a true sense of self-love and love of other which is our human and divine condition and destiny before God.

Steps towards resolution of Ethnic conflicts

There is much that could be said about the nature of conflict in different countries throughout the world and in those differing situations, each people may need to do several things namely to agree to accept that conflicts of the past, especially the distant past, be left where they belong, in history, not forgotten, but de-sensitised so that they can no longer control their mindset, to agree that all parties wish to live in peace for the sake of their families and neighbours, and with each other, to agree to be bound be the highest and most honourable practices in public life, to agree to work together to attain a standard of living for each party which is just and fair, to set in motion a dialogue which addresses concerns or disputes from either party, regarding issues such as territory, inequality, protection of culture/identity, infrastructure and environment and to agree to enshrine in the way of life the spiritual and aspirational values of the each people.

Resolutions on the cauldron of middle-Eastern conflict

We need only consider the state of strife in Syria and neighbouring middle-Eastern states in 2013, to recognise the frightful ferocity which can result from ethnic and religious differences and aspirations, and the very great need that there is to persuade the many different parties that there is a more accommodating way forward. I suggest that trying to recognise the reasons for the dissent can be temptation to falling into the trap of being entrenched with the grievances, rather than pointing a way out of the mire which is acceptable to all.

Considering the nature of dissent and conflict in Syria, as a throbbing and exceedingly painful example of ethoses in conflict, we must recognise that the origins of the different factions there can be found, historically, in the Syrian's regime's interdependence on Russia in recent generations, the loyalties which have ensued, the allegiance between the current Syrian regime with such a power in the region as Iran, together with traditional Shia/Sunni frictions.

Unfortunately the added thorn in the Syrian situation is that it has been used by Al-Qaeda and all kinds of associated foreign fundamentalist terrorists, on the backs of local rebels, as a vehicle for pursuit of radical Islamic fundamentalism in the whole of the Middle Eastern region. Syria became the central and foremost location for this struggle, after extremists were forced from such countries as Afghanistan and Iraq. History will judge whether it has been prudent for western nations to ignore the fact that it has been Jihadists who have aggravated the vicious and merciless war in Syria on the backs of the local Syrian people, who were already reasonably peaceful with their secular, multi-faithed society, and whether the West mis-judged the alliance of Russia, the Assad regime and Iran as being the greater of two evils in an involved and ingrained conflict, largely in the competition for superiority between Sunni and Shia in the wider range of Middle-Eastern countries. Undoubtedly there have been undesirably violent episodes on both sides, but the nature of the beast in the core of the Middle-Eastern countries, with the drive by extremists toward Islamic fundamentalism and Sharia law, is that violent repercussions are almost unavoidable, and all parties can be guilty of atrocities, but it is the question of which can be judged as the greater of two evils.

Additionally there is the Israeli/Palestinian issue, which might be handled and settled as a separate issue, provided that most Palestinian concerns can be addressed. The core concern in 2013 has been the rise of vicious, merciless Jihadist extremism in the Middle-East, against the wishes of the vast majority of people in their own countries. Other countries throughout the world must not lose sight of, or be seduced by, the core aggravating factor of aggressive Islamic fundamentalism, and thereby punish those who are trying to fight it, each in their own way. The West must not be seen to have been blind to the greater implications of backing the wrong party in Syria, thereby inviting war-footing with Russia, China and Iran.

What IS required of all parties, and especially, in this case Russia and Iran, and also the Western powers of US, Britain etc, is honest and open pronouncements in the public, international arena, which are based on an honest, compassionate, reconciliatory and forward-looking approach, which can heal old enmities and scores, hold Islamic extremism to account, and which is inspired by the will of God which is to live together in universal harmony, rather than to, in the name of religion, be at each other's throats.

In all cases, it is distinctly possible that countries in a state of conflict will need assistance and aid from outside in order to put these steps in place, not least from other nations who have already been through this transition successfully. Much assistance can also be given by the developed world as a result of 'intellectual property' on conflict resolution, dialogue, development and peace.

The vital component of charismatic and inspired leadership

We must recognise that it is primarily the tenacity and vision of individuals in positions of influence and local power, who can and must effect this movement towards accommodation. The realisation of the Peace Process in N Ireland was only possible because of the participation of wise, far-sighted and tenacious individuals in the political arena, who will go down in history for their attainment of some of the noblest aims in public and political life.

In a spiritual context, it might also be realised that the contribution of individual souls in realising such peace is in fact a very Godly task, the will of God and, I suggest, realisation of our universal ethos.

12

The Islam Imperative

Let us consider the fundamental reasons behind the evidence of Muslim statements of objection to the western capitalist philosophy. We can be in little doubt of the reality of this stance, as evidenced so poignantly by those whose lives have been lost or affected in the violent exchanges between the ideologies. We need to have a true understanding of the causes of this dissension.

There are core feelings within the Muslim nations of peoples which currently confound western philosophy. While I am not an expert on these fundamental beliefs and differences, I can only speak from observation and attempt an understanding of what appears to be evident, namely that the Muslim peoples, and in particular their men, have a strong belief in the importance of expressing their alignment with their divine identity under the statutes of the Koran and their divinity, Mohammed, by the way they live their lives and by the way their society is conducted. Their strength of purpose is arguably as strong, if not stronger, than that held by any other ideology, hence their determination and self-sacrifice even to the point of death for what they believe to be correct. They are in disdain of what they see as corruptness or deviance from character in other ideologies, primarily those of western capitalism and they harbour resentment and defiance towards the supposition of moral, economic, philosophical and military superiority of western capitalist democracy. Whether the resolve of jihadists to bring violent introduction of Sharia law to the rest of the world, is a plausible cause, is disputable. While we must take account of the vehemence of these objecting peoples, we must also be aware that there may be many people/men who conscribe to this ideology who are part of it, more because of their own violent and dissenting natures and as such constitute a very dangerous tendency. Also there can be many practices amongst radical zealots, not least in their perspective towards women, which represent a severe rebuttal of very primary humane values. It must also be borne in mind that, despite the aggressive jihadist response to western liberalism, there is a very large percentage of Muslim people who are quietly, inoffensively and strongly faithful to their religious faith, admirable in their way of life and a threat to no-one. That fact must be more greatly publicised, as these many peoples abide by a loving and pious way of life. It must be borne in mind that all people, whatever their origins have indefatigable needs and rights to be allowed to conduct their life in a manner conducive to their spiritual well-being, true to their cultural origins and in hope of their spiritual dream.

It is also a subject for review that, following such events as 9/11, that perhaps if western forces had taken on board some self-examination of flagrant western capitalist ways and resolved that, in the interests of our universal nature, they might hear what dissenting Arab dissidents were saying, and temper the grossly offensive aspects of flagrant western practices, then this may have been a much more prudent step in the interests of universal ethos, than immediate military retaliation. Only history will reveal what the better path might have been, however it is gratifying that in the interim time, western governments have visibly become more self-correcting in their approach to international dissension and policy, as a result of the punishment inflicted upon them. It might only be said that the nett affect has tentatively been greater steps towards realisation of a better universal state.

As in any argument or disagreement on fundamental issues of the meaning of life, it is essential that we understand the reasons for dissension and succeed in agreeing statutes which are true to the wholesome spirit of man, which honours and respects our common universal needs. It is all the more essential now that we have come to blows on the issues, which can seriously threaten the peace and security of our world.

A mistaken assumption of superiority by one ideology over another can culminate in imposing uniformity, sometimes named globalisation, which, in effect, is a subtle imposition of sameness, which both numbs the idea of organic self-realisation by cultures, and denies us all of the unique flavours which different cultures have to offer of themselves.

Instead of this, the quality of love and tolerance in action must support different peoples in realising their own organic beauty, while in the process of addressing the basic universal needs, desires and intuitions for expressing that sense of order in life which is the natural state of our human drive and destiny. Co-incident with this state of play, is the need for statutes to be drawn up between nations, which, wisely, define the basic needs and rights of the human spirit, and to agree to honour the details of these statutes in our relations and international relations with each other.

13

Territorial and Ethnic disputes

Is it not true that most political conflicts throughout the world, through all ages, have been due to disputes over territorial ownership and/or ethnic/religious dominance. Is it not also true, that as human beings, despite all our knowledge of diplomacy, we continue to find these conflicts, almost intractable. Is it not time for both parties, in such an arena of conflict, to adopt a strategy where understanding is given to the cause of the dispute. In many cases, the violations have been by force by more dominant races. Perhaps there are fundamental principles which need to be initiated in order to resolve these often catastrophic disputes, namely acknowledgement, by the ruling people, of the offensiveness caused, and the possible invalidity of their holding of the disputed territory, and secondly, acknowledgement by all parties, that the place where we live, is home, we should be glad to have it, and we need to agree to honour each other's identity here where we live.

We must all recall that a large percentage of any population have their place of abode governed more by their economic state than by their desire. It is almost certain that most of us, in our lives, have needed to make our home, even for a limited period, in a place, perhaps in another country, under another jurisdiction, which we would not chose ideally, because of work, place of study, financial constraint etc ? Is it not also true that what becomes important in these instances, is that we are able to have our primary needs met, and we have the opportunity to make new friends in this location, by sharing and co-operation ? It is not therefore a vital requirement, in conditions of conflict, that all parties accept to make themselves at home where they are, without hankering after the territory of which they feel they have been deprived, provided the next criterion is met ? Namely, acknowledgment and agreement, by the now resident party, that the territory will be completely open for travel, purchase of property, fully participating residence by the displaced people, and that statutes are written into the constitution of that territory, which give dual citizenship to all individuals who wish it, that the ruling party will always be above party politics, and contain equal representation of all ethnic origins resident with a claim to the territory, thereby ensuring that all individuals may practice their ethnic/spiritual life privately, while, in daily life, they contribute within the laws of agreed honourable and steadfast statutes, for the common good of all. Thereby each may allude to their own nationhood, while expecting to be treated with human equality, by all those who rule their country.

Governments with accountability

It would be a requisite of the new society, that a person may be assigned to a position of leadership or responsibility, only if he/she is above party politics, and completely endorse the principle of the universal spirit.

It is interesting to note that, in our present society, this would preclude a large percentage of people who are currently in political life and positions of responsibility in working life, sadly mostly in political life.

It is from this topic, that we envisage the need for stringent changes in the criteria for acceptability at all levels of political life, and also at all levels of responsibility in working life. It is the former which is in most need of addressing.

It would be necessary, for legislation to be brought in which would guarantee binding of political individuals to have to perform above party politics. By these statutes, positions in political life would be applied for, much like in working life, and the tasks would be performed much like in other walks of working life. There would no longer be a place for party politics.

How much of our time, attention and intellectual resources are taken up, contending with the conflicting, and so often unnecessary arguments, propounded by party politicians. It is an insult to human intellect and spirit and, arguably, a criminal misappropriation of public funds resources and accountability. It should be outlawed accordingly.

In the same way that companies world-wide, are successfully governed, guided and restrained by their ruling bodies, to the point of success for all their employees, and within all constraints of the law, the same should now apply for those who work to organise the running of a country.

It is then, also, a desirable and probably necessary requirement that agreement is come to, between countries, on a global level, of the statutes and standards to be attained and maintained within their legal systems, in accordance with the universal spirit, and that International Bodies such as the UN, NATO etc require that all countries who wish to be part of this international allegiance have these clearly-defined statutes enshrined in the international code of Practice. These statutes, based on moral, ethical, honourable, steadfast and legal grounds would have to be agreed by all the member states, perhaps with disputes on route so as to deduce the best way forward for all. Once agreed and established, all states would have to prove their worthiness to be part of this body, by stringent rulings regarding such issues in governmental life as legal correctness, absence of any corruption in public life, and fairness in administrative governance. Any countries not meeting these stringent criteria would have to be encouraged by such incentives as disadvantage for not being members, in order to require them to rise to the necessary stringent standards in public life. It is a travesty that in the present state of the world, while there have been many leading countries in the past 200 yrs, mainly leading democracies in the West such as Britain, France, Germany, USA etc, who have set the benchmark for such fair and just statutes for the world, that there are still such a large number of countries, including large economic players like the BRIC countries, who demonstrably fail to attain anywhere close to the necessary requirements on fairness, lack of corruption and honourable practice.

Is it not totally realisable that, in those countries where strife and internal conflicts exist, global commercial companies are doing exactly what it is that we now require of governments, hence it is totally realisable, by diplomatic efforts and agreement.

Model for national, international and world leadership

It is an interesting fact to note that the only model we have for global co-operation is one of agreement between equals at the highest levels, that is to say, we don't have a World Leader. The closest to this that we have is the current position of the President of the United States, as the leader of the world's largest economy and primary democracy. And it is possible that that position could change in the foreseeable future to a country such as China. This evidences the need for agreement on all issues pertaining to our world, by the leaders of the participating, and often the most prominent, nations. There is no master, only an allegiance of, we hope, wise leaders.

At least, as a starting point, we do have the correct structure in place, which emulates perhaps the fundamental principle of the universal spirit, that is mutual recognition and alliance on our common needs, and innate wisdom.

However it must be said that elected world leaders have undeniable and unparalleled opportunity to say words of ultimate wisdom to lead, direct, appease fears of not only their own people, but those of the rest of the world. These leaders incorporate all national leaders, and religious figures including the Pope and the Dalai Lama and it is their unique opportunity, and incumbent upon them, to be reflective on every issue, to allow themselves to be inspired by divine guidance and to ALWAYS and AT EVERY OPPORTUNITY speak words of wisdom, guidance and discernment, which are beyond the petty recriminations of Man, and in search of the ultimate truth. There is enough guidance in all our Holy books to allow great leaders to step aside from confusing scenarios and renew the implanting of Godly ways in all our affairs, personal, national and international. This is the ultimate guidance to which we must always resort and strive for.

Section 4

Ecology and Economy

14

Finance and Banking

As a result of the world economic collapse of 2008/9, it is abundantly clear that the current model of western capitalism is inadequate for the people of the world, for the present or the future. This document suggests strategies which must change in order to facilitate mankind in establishing a life-style for all which acknowledges our basic human needs, disposition and destiny on our journey through life. It deals, first of all, with the long term strategies suggested primarily for the future and the peoples of the future, and also with suggested immediate strategies to facilitate recovery from the current world economic stalemate.

Primary reasons for Economic and Environmental Rethink

At this stage in mankind's history and especially over the most recent half-century, the people of the world are using, at too high a rate, non-renewable resources and are too driven by consuming rather than renewing, whereby due and necessary consideration is not being given for peoples of the future. The established model of capitalism is too heavily weighted on profit, consuming and growth, at the expense of equilibrium with the natural world. Much of the western-style capitalist world is too driven by the incessant need to develop to new technological levels, which cannot continue indefinitely at its current rate as there is little left to be developed or discovered. Humankind may need to come to terms with living a humbler, simpler life where we work to live, have a less rushed life and have more opportunity for quality time with family and friends, participating in the best things in life which are free. There are many developed countries which function well in many of these areas however there are also examples of countries where daily life tends to be driven by the rat-race mentality. Perhaps this was more so before the financial crisis of recent years and is less so, more by imposition, since the onset of economic retardation.

Core quantitative areas of concern

It is our reality that the world's population has grown at an alarming rate in recent decades and might continue to grow at a similar rate, for which current plans and world resources cannot provide. Also because of raised population levels, and highly automated ways of manufacturing, there are not, and will not, be enough jobs to keep people gainfully employed with an acceptable income. It is arguable that the world cannot continue to grow indefinitely in technological development, in the way that it has in the past century. In fact it is possible that there can be virtually no more growth, when we look at the complexity of technology available to us all in all aspects of life and work achieved presently. Therefore the future may need to be of a humbler lifestyle, where our basic needs are met and qualities of love and caring predominate.

An additional quantitative area of concern is that the current mode of capitalism allows for flagrant borrowing at the higher echelons of the financial world, such as countries, international conglomerates and big business, which allows the 'top-heavy' wallowing of finance to be inherently unstable and liable to being out of control, which is what happened in the World economic crisis of 2008/9 and since. Also the tools used by financial houses to invest in the stock and money markets are excessively too complex and risky and need to be de-complicated by regulation, to methods which are predictable and realisable. There is too much freedom for too much capital to be held by a few, whereby it is not being used efficiently for the good of the economy/society/the under-privileged and those at the bottom of the economic ladder are becoming too many and too poor.

We are the custodians of the future for all future peoples of the world ! Thereby, we must put in place ecological and economic policies which are sustainable for ALL of the future.

Higher World Capital Reserves and Tax Changes

It is becoming more and more evident that an area of financial regulation which may need to be remodelled is that of tax revenue gathering, nationally and internationally. There may be many different ways of looking at the advantages or disadvantages of differing rules regarding tax liabilities, including nationally and across borders. As much of our global economy revolves around large conglomerates which can have vast revenues, it is suggested that, especially for those larger conglomerates, there be, perhaps, simpler but more stringent regulation, nationally and internationally, which requires larger percentages of overall profits to be submitted as taxes, above an acceptable minimum level, to central funds for example IMF and World Bank, on something of a 'pawn-broker model', as a means of creating much greater capital available in reserve for any and all types of world crises. The reason for the 'pawn-broker' method is so as to mean that contributing organisations can think of the higher percentage of contribution not so much as being lost to taxes but instead 'set aside for a rainy day'. The purpose of these greatly enhanced world funds would be manifold, namely as a buffer against future world economic crises, as aid/loans to needy developing countries, as loans at normal rates to growing businesses as they grow and expand the economy, and, crucially now additionally, to contributing companies at highly competitive rates. This possibility of 'lending-back' of funds will mean that the contributing organisations can maintain their incentives to do well, so as to keep very much alive the incentives for entrepreneurialism, while leaving the discretion to the large world fund holders to make funds available in the case of crises or crisis-hit areas, so as to dampen or prevent the kind of economic collapses that our current free-market capitalism has enabled, so catastrophically by the farcical boom and bust mentality. It will be necessary to set the levels of these higher taxes carefully to maintain a balance so that the incentive is still there to produce highly, and to encourage competition between countries to come up with, and be successful in, producing alternatives to the big blue-chip suppliers, whereby these areas of business development are areas where greatest remuneration can still be achieved, to promote entrepreneurialism and success.

Reining in of international tax rules

Another area of tax management which it is abundantly clear needs correcting and clarifying on a large scale, is the arena of international tax liabilities for companies operating in several countries. It is becoming widely evident that billions of dollars are being lost to a country's tax revenues by greedy conglomerates who reap the profits for themselves, by making use of inadequate or lax tax rules, and countries which are tax havens. This practice must be outlawed. Modification of this tax legislation would require international agreement, but I think the first primary step that must be taken is in recognising that it is within each country that a company operates, that the local tax system must demand that any work done in that country, must be liable to taxation in accordance with the nature and scale of that work. Take, for example, a global company, say founded in USA, which does sales of products on-line in the UK, and the products are shipped from, say, the Netherlands. Then the company must first of all establish, under new audited and declared rules, what percentage of the sale activity is attributed in each country. For example if this products are manufactured in US, marketing and on-line sales done in UK and shipment done from Netherlands, then the tax liability in each country will be in proportion to the cost and scale of the exercise in that country. In such an instance, the greatest cost involved may be the manufacture, the next greatest cost, transport, storage and shipment from Netherlands, and the next greatest cost, online marketing and order processing. These percentages must be established by law in the country of incorporation and head office of the company, in this case USA. It may still remain the case that different countries have widely differing tax rates, and companies may choose to have offices to perform different functions in different countries, but the scale of tax liability MUST NOW, by law, be in proportion to the scale and cost of the activity in that country, and not simply be used as a corridor for evading taxes, as it now so flagrantly is. It is a fact that companies may currently not be breaking any laws and that is only because such tax regulations as the above are not in place for them to abide me. This must surely change.

Banks and Lending financial institutions

The above are the steps necessary to rationalise public funds, managing the revenues of international companies, in their tax on profits and fiscal responsibilities. Now we must consider the bindings which need to be placed on banks and financial institutions regarding the lending of money in prudent ways. Initially let us look at the function of the High St banks, whose everyday business is loans and savings. There will be 3 strands to the requirement upon them, the first being the requirement on banks to hold a much higher percentage of capital against all loans, the second being greatly reduced interdependence between banks, including internationally, and thirdly much greater risk assessment on parties to be lent to. It will also be highly desirable to split off the Lending and Savings arms of the big banks from their Investment arms, so that risk to High St customers is averted in the case of unwise investments by the investment arms of the banks. The main requirement on both High St and Investment arms will now be to greatly rein in and obliterate much of the complexity of borrowing and, until now, high-risk investment tools.

The lending and investment practices of the banks will not become more boring, but less interdependent, much simpler and much more risk averse. Keeping it simpler and more secure is the only sane way to go forward, for the financial world and for all our sakes.

15

Economy

Economics in a nutshell

The wheels of economics might be summarised into the following. A country has natural wealth in the form of food, other renewables and raw materials of the earth. Different countries obviously have diverse differences in these facets. In addition to these sources of wealth, for their own population and for export, there are added-value 'products' for export in the form of ingenuity, scientific and other intellectual property. These are the vehicles of the economy. The purpose of the economy in each country must be towards a much higher national level of self-sufficiency in food and materials, by optimising value-added products for export, to create a positive trade deficit and an aim to run the country with zero or negligible borrowing.

Countries must now run on these principles, so as to be able to accumulate wealth and be able to afford such vital public services as health, welfare, transport defence etc. ie to maintain a positive budget deficit.

If a country cannot afford, by its renewables and raw materials to maintain its own population, then it is highly likely that populations will gradually shift to countries where larger populations can be sustained. In addition to aid needing to be provided to these countries to help them optimise their productivity, migration may need to be facilitated but this must be done in a controlled, manageable and sustainable way. The current trend of masses of populations moving from one country to another because of shortcomings in their own country, must be tempered, addressed and facilitation given to improving development to acceptable international standards.

The Labour Market

It is an unavoidable reality that the world's population is increasing at unprecedented levels and at the present time, it has more than doubled in the past half-century, from what it has been for the whole of the world's history prior to then ! It is possible that this is unsustainable, but in any event, if the global population does continue to increase at current levels, then the figures could prove to be unmanageable. There are obviously many implications of this, not least regarding food supply, but the issue which we want to look at at present is that of work possibilities. An additional factor demographically with regard to work is that it is a result of our highly evolved technological attainment, much work has been replaced by machines and automation rendering many people unemployed or underemployed. We need only open our eyes to the figures for unemployment in some countries in Europe presently, say Spain where adult unemployment is 25% and unemployment amongst young people is over 50% ! One wonders if many such people are suffering in silence as this is an unsustainable and unbearable state. We would be wearing blinkers to fail to see this inevitable reality and will need to be pragmatic and realistic about taking measures to take account of it. While there may be different ways of going about addressing this probable reduction in jobs worldwide, one possible strategy, and this is only one, might be to encourage greater presence of women working in the home and in caring roles including the professions eg medicine, health care, with the men going out to all other regular jobs. This is not by any means a suggestion to limit the possibilities of women working in any profession, merely a recognition of typical female qualities with their disposition towards caring. While allowing for females with strong attributes in many other fields, perhaps a larger percentage might be in caring roles. One other reason why the 'caring professions' may need to be much more prevalent, is the inevitable fact that, with greatly improved health care, the percentage of the population who are aging, beyond working age and in need of care for a longer time, will necessitate a much larger percentage of people working, whether paid or as charity, in the fields of caring. For these reasons in our economic reality regarding longer term underemployment globally, and rapidly increased needs for caring roles, it may mean that fewer women may be in traditional paid jobs, but instead by occupied in local conglomerate activity and caring roles, for which acceptable remuneration is established by combination of contribution from spouse and or/ benefits. It will be mandatory to legislate for adequate minimum income/household where there is not a working man to provide that eg. Single women, broken relationships, widows/widowers and other singles.

Work to live rather than live to work

It would be desirable to induce in mankind, the mentality to tend towards work and a life-style which does not require unnecessary excess head-work where not required, where physical work is good for the mind and there is more opportunity for restfulness, social activity, fun and relaxation in free time. Those of inherently high intelligence will continue do the jobs which require such abilities such eg. Medicine, engineering design, scientific research, economics. Thereby it should be possible and desirable to reduce the % of people going to conventional university and increase the % going to occupational colleges and training schools, as I believe that many, many students are currently being required to acquire much academic knowledge which is probably superfluous, with attendant stress, strain and unnecessary distressing competition for the many young people involved. This undesirable competition and costs involved may submit our young people to some horrendous pressures, which may often be carried silently and damagingly for their lives and for the future which is an unacceptable situation. It would be ideal to encourage the lifestyle amongst all people where work is run-of-the-mill without the unnecessary rat-race activity, and where leisure time encourages social fun and serenity/equilibrium with the natural world as the be-all and end-all.

16

Ecology and Agriculture

Environmental Strategies
Energy and Renewables

It will be necessary to drastically reduce consumption of throw-away products worldwide, reduce to approaching 0% of carbon fuel consumption, directly and for electricity production. Instead increase to 100% geothermal, renewable and perhaps nuclear, under strict safety standards, for generation of electricity and for heating. It will also be necessary to greatly increase the level of recyclability towards 100% globally, to greatly increase the fuel efficiency of homes and buildings, to legislate for the switching off of power eg lighting in big businesses, during out of hours worldwide. Other highly desirable aims will be to reduce housing costs to sensible, manageable financial levels, perhaps to take 80-90% of carbon-fuelled vehicles off the road, to greatly increase the % of electric cars for local journeys. There could be incentives to increase public transport to 90% for longer journeys, utilising electric vehicles at destination, with encouragement to walk to public transport, locally. It could be advisable to reduce drastically the amount of travelling over long distances nationally and internationally, enabling and supporting travel between countries only or primarily to sell intellectual services to other countries to assist in their internal development to acceptable internal and international levels.

Agriculture and Food Production

In order make much greater use of abundant agricultural land in each country where this can be facilitated, create radical new infrastructure of local agricultural production centres in satellite form around urban centres, small and large, which make provision of field-grown produce eg fruit and veg, animal stock for dairy and meat production and poly-tunnels for fruit/veg which need high solar input. These units would supply local markets/supermarkets, using regulation re quality etc. already in place, in addition to being available for purchase directly by the public at reduced cost, subsidised if necessary for those on minimum income. These local centres would be in addition to current agricultural mass production methods and supermarket arrangements with all current regulation already in place. The idea is that these centres would be within walking distance, and be places where those on limited employment, some ill/disabled and pensioners could find gainful activity. They could be economical sources of foodstuffs for those who need to economise and promoting local social interaction and support. Another aim might be to greatly increase the percentage of people employed in agriculture/food production area.

What to do from this point in current World Economic stalemate

What follows is a short analysis of the current world economic predicament since 2008/9, how it might be possible to reduce the stalemate, and stimulate recovery.

The current world economic crisis, arguably one of the worst in the history of mankind, came about in 2008/9, largely as a result of the flagrant and inadequately regulated global financial practices allowed, for which the above recommendations attempt a solution for now and for the future.

Some of the main consequences of the crash have been that vast quantities of money have changed hands from financial institutions to private recipients, as a result of flagrant lending. Thus the financial institutions/banks/countries were effectively broke, causing massive squeeze on government and welfare spending, and reduced world demand producing slowed or negative growth even in productive countries. Thus much capital now exists in private hands, and is being largely unproductive as a result of hesitant stock market activity and low interest rates. Much 'hypothetical' wealth which existed in inflated stocks has evaporated. A necessary solution would be to tempt the private capital to invest in strategies which would bring about balanced growth. This would require the leading governments and leaders in the world to announce putting in place strategies such as those suggested in this article, to 'reassure potential investors'.

So many in the developed world, now feel the pinch of austerity in addition to all those others in the 2nd and 3rd worlds who never knew anything else. Now is the time to institute an economy for modest living on grounds which are economically and ecologically sound, and to put in place strategies and legislation which would be the bedrock of this new economic outlook.

Primary economic steps to reduce heat in the crisis

This could be a primary building block for initiating recovery.

For those home and property owners who were stung by the massive fall in property prices since 2008/9, especially for those who purchased around the peak of the market, their debt for the inflated values of these properties should be 'wiped-out', rendering those property owners with enhanced expendable income at this time. A newly-coined term for this, often in use now, is debt forgiveness and is becoming a more realistic proposition for consideration as a means of rebalancing serious debt and credit variances. The financial lenders of these loans will have to take the hit, therefore financially will be at a low ebb, thus shares in these companies will be at rock-bottom prices, there will be more expendable income in the population, therefore more economic activity, making everyone a little richer, with the obvious knock-on effects of an improved property market, thereby improving the capital of the mortgage companies and providing returns for their investors. Thereby the property market and the wider economy would become more active.

A side-effect of this mortgage strategy is that the value of the properties is at a much more modest level, for example that of perhaps 10-12 yrs ago, which is as it should be.

With newly-instituted, much more conservative lending practices now by banks/financial institutions, property will now only be allowed to grow at a very modest rate. The days of 'get-rich-quick' for every Tom, Dick and Harry will be over, but a modest, more stable and more contented life can ensue.

With property values much reduced, wages/salaries will no longer need to be forced up to meet requirements and the household budget will remain modest.

Costs of Food and Energy

For a household to reduce its expenditure, if housing costs are reduced, now other costs eg consumables must be addressed, primarily food and energy.

The aim to make housing energy costs approach zero carbon must be accelerated. In developed countries, strategies for this are already well-accelerated, but will need to be progressed. Obviously, for infrastructure reasons, many properties may not have the facilities for zero carbon production. In these cases, the strategy will be to reduce energy consumption to the minimum possible. There will be hurdles to be overcome, as different areas of the world will have different needs/attributes in this regard.

Re travel, the strategies detailed in this document need to be followed, regarding reducing carbon fuel usage. Thereby, there will need to be more electric vehicles for local travel and public transport operating to full capacity, for longer journeys, subsidised if necessary to greatly encourage usage. Thereby costs to the user will be greatly reduced.

With energy costs coming more and more from renewable electricity sources, the cost of these to the user will become increasing less as the years, decades and generations proceed.

Costs for Food

Re food, let us remind ourselves that when we talk about 'growth' in the economy, it is arguable that the only growth required for mankind is food, which is completely renewable, provided we have a roof over our heads ! If we all had enough space, we could be totally self-sufficient, with virtually zero costs for food. That is unrealistic for 100% of the world's population as a high % of people are urban-dwellers, but the reality still remains that basic food production can approach zero cost, with nominal payment to the producer for growing costs and slight profit !

Thereby costs to the average household for food should not be excessive.

Other essential costs to the household

Other primary costs to a household are clothing, other consumables eg cleaning products, essential insurance cover typically house, contents, life, health, vehicle, phones and broadband, home contents incl electrical/computing which should be one-off purchases renewed as infrequently as every 10/20 years. Only clothing/educational equipment above will be higher where there are children in the household. The number of children which a family could have, might well have to be tempered by the parents' ability to provide for them by their income.

Other non-essential household costs

With more modest economic earnings, there will be luxuries which households may no longer be able to afford. And so be it. Foreign holidays may become a rarer event for the majority.

It is probable that mankind will benefit enormously from living in a more modest way, where the best quality of life is in the home with loved ones, and the free enjoyment of socialisation locally and with friends in already-established sophisticated premises and facilities is adequate re-creation for most. The people of the world need to rediscover that the best things in life are free and come from a balanced equilibrium with the natural world. The secret in achieving this is to be able to establish bodies which can agree to this worldwide.

International agreements on such strategies

Through such organisations as United Nations, it would be possible to legislate for all the countries of the world to subscribe to the above principles, so as to enable sustainability within each country, help for those countries in need, encouragement for a healthy minimum-to-moderate competitiveness amongst countries so as to keep standards high and the entrepreneurial spirit actively alive, as incentive to excellence.

In addition to all of above, and as controlling factors, it will be necessary to institute international financial rules which control world and human activity to moderate and sustainable, rather than frenetic levels, with low-risk financial activity accompanied by high capital reserves and generous rules regarding financing of countries at basic and intermediate stages of development. It would be necessary to make these agreements through International bodies amongst the vast majority of subscribing countries, who then gain proportionate benefit and as incentive to other countries who have not signed up so as to encourage membership so as to gain from the positive benefits and stability of belonging.

Renewed outlook on life

With renewed economic and environmental constraints for mankind, perhaps new directions and mottos for mankind could be working to live rather than living to work, making the aim of worldly life to feed, house and protect one's family, to care and be accountable for each other in home and society, to encourage a healthy balance of work with home-life/leisure time and social/relaxation time and to attend to our spiritual needs in the passage through life.

Section 5

The Way Forward

17

Primary and Secondary Needs

It may be worthwhile taking a critical look at what are really the primary things which we most need in life, if there were a limit of resources, as there is for two-thirds of the world's population already.

Simply Living

What are your primary needs, for day-to-day living ? The answers I find to this are a roof over one's head, source of heat/fire, water, food, hygienic way to dispose of personal waste, detergent and vessels, somewhere warm and soft to lay one's head at night and opportunity to use one's mind and my body to daily ensure these needs are met and to help facilitate our neighbour to do the same. It is a reality, which those of in the west perhaps don't have to take much time to reflect on, that the vast majority of people in our world have to think this way on a daily basis. God forbid that any of us should be thrust into a situation like this, by, for instance a natural disaster such as an earthquake or tsunami. It should therefore not be beyond us to consider the possible implications of being in such a situation. Meeting of these needs are fundamental for any human being, and it may be pertinent to remind ourselves that the needs of all other human beings are fundamentally the same.

Why, then, do two thirds of the population of the universe, as we know it, seem to have none of these needs assured on a daily basis ? Your inner voice of reason must now surely start to make your mind and body determine to attempt to rectify this situation ? Do you have reason to be joyful, at the end of each day, if you have company with whom you can share that both of you have had your needs met for that day ? Then is it not your desire to set about ensuring that all other people on this planet, and with whom you share the universe, also have this experience at the end of each day ?

Secondary Needs

If your primary needs are met, what might be other critical needs which exist. The answers may be clothing, medical care and antidotes to causes of disease, procreation and perhaps the wheel ?

There are things which we do not vitally need, but can utilise for the sake of ourselves and our fellow human-beings. They would include long-distance travel vehicles, radio and satellite communications, aesthetically-pleasing lotions/potions or cosmetics, refined metal/plastic products for daily use and heavy-duty functions.

It may seem trite to be reviewing such basic commodities, but we must consider the rest of our fellow human beings who are at many and varied points along the scale of achieving many of these things.

The Human Population and the World's resources

Much could be said on the subject of the world's material resources and in particular on the subject of the urgency for vastly increasing the scale of renewables and recyclables, but perhaps suffice to say, at this point, that we need to re-evaluate the raw material needs and supply of them, for all the peoples of the world as a whole. We need to agree the extraction of natural resources, from wherever they are, by agreement with the people of those countries, in view of environmental constraints, in balance with full capacity for recyclables, in view of the modest needs of mankind and taking into account adequate remuneration to the countries of supply. Much more may be said on this topic in future accounts.

18

Journey of life through the ages

It is an indefatigable reality that each of us born to this earth has a journey from conception, through birth, through infancy, childhood, growing up through the many stages of adulthood and ultimately through old age, for most, and on to death, with which we all have to grapple. For most there are many challenges, hurdles to get over, trials, as well, obviously as joy, well-being, success, love and harmony. However it is the reality that we all have to travel this journey, a journey not of our own making, but that of our parents and by the hand of God. It is therefore incumbent upon us to recognise our value and that of all others as a sentient and spiritual entity, which deserves to be understood and supported in our journey through life.

As we recall our experiences through the different stages of life, we might ponder on the times when we have felt contained and enwrapped in love, where nothing is a problem and anything is possible. As instructed by spiritual and religious teaching, that is the condition of love, love of self, love of other, love of God. However in addition to these memories many of us recall having times of struggle perhaps at the different stages of life. Perhaps that journey through life has been daunting at times, perhaps a road we have to travel whether we like it or not. Perhaps that time has been during childhood, adolescence or adulthood and it reminds us that there can be difficulties for our human condition. This is true no more so than for people who have some form of illness or disability, whose human experience feels less than perfect. That may somehow seem unacceptable to those whose life seems much more honky-dory, but it makes us realise that the most important facet of our human reality is our capacity to have happiness, joy, compassion, love and communication. And, after all, these are the aspects which our God, whoever that may be to us, asks and requires of us. That is our spiritual reality. In addition to those who have difficulties through life, there are situations where the young die early. Sometimes this may seem unacceptable or unnecessary. Therein we are shown that what matters in our destiny is the sense of love that we attain before God, for self and other that we establish in life, not the length of our life, and hopefully this can help to come to terms with an early death. As we proceed through life, also we might become physically or mentally less able and have to come to terms with the fact that we are not all-powerful, but instead the best that we can do is to share well-being and have empathy for others. This again is part of us fulfilling our destiny to be a loving entity, a reality which we share with all our other fellow human-beings. It reminds us of our capacity and duty to be a successful and contributing part of the universal ethos, so that hopefully when our time comes to finally leave this world, we can say that we have always tried to add to the feeling of universal spirit of goodness before God. It is true that of all the faiths and religions that we have throughout our world, the general stipulations and expectations are largely the same. It is arguable that any differences that we all have are things that can be talked about to come to an understanding, thereby undoing the differences that we have. God grant that that is the task that we set ourselves , so as, in the words of St Francis of Assisi, to bring harmony where there is discord, hope where there is despair and peace at the last.

Yoga and Meditation as support for spirituality

I have found no other medium so intrinsically conducive to the true and good natural experience of personal physical, mental, emotional and spiritual well-being. I have found it to be subtle, simple and profound and in its most basic experience, can dissolve the many barriers, conflicts and competitions which exist within our other life practices, in a flash, replacing them with a peaceful, open, accepting, resolving and clear aspect to life and to one another, at one and the same time enhancing our clarity for the resolution of difference and the achievement of perfection. Its subtle, enduring profundity cannot easily be understood by those who have never practised it, and yet it is so easy and virtually effortless to make this happen.

My summary of the effects of Yoga would be total self-acceptance and self-love, thereby facilitating the mutual application of that to each other. It is so simple and so enduringly profound. I believe that, from a spiritual or religious perspective, yoga or similar meditative methods are tools which under-pin our physical and mental well-being in such a way that we are in a better state to realise our spiritual identity, to be open to the restful, peaceful and harmonious aspects of our human reality, able to share this with others in love, in place of the many distracting and busy things which occupy our lives, and thereby realising our capacity to love and our spiritual identity before God, whoever we may think our God to be. I believe this spiritual well-being and identity to be the fundamental basis of our universal spirit, and our pre-eminent destiny in God.

It might also be suggested that irrespective of who our many religions think our God is, He is only the One God who looks down upon all of us, and hopes to gather us all to Himself fulfilled through our work in life in His likeness and image and in love with one another.

But what must be said is that in achieving this true trust and growth under a common universal ethos for humanity, it is fundamental that our stance be steadfast, truthful, honourable, unflinching and eternal, until all peace between nations is achieved.

19

Renewing our Direction

At this point in our history, where so much has already been achieved to better our way of living, from technological developments to medical practice, and democratic procedures to ensure every manner of equanimity in our society, it is now time that we take stock of the damage that the frenetic speed of development has had on environment and human spirit alike, now and for the future. We must now rise to the challenge of affirming our commitment to each other in a common moral ethos, which seeks to protect all primary human need, our greatest values and our ecology together, by effecting the primary steps necessary to find the way forward for attaining harmony in our world. As so much has been attained and yes there are errors, this process is like something akin to redirecting a fast-moving and large momentum train. As such, the good news is that it is largely on the right track, and the gratifyingly good news is that, because much of what is achieved is pointing in the right direction, redirection will be largely a matter of 'tweaking' the systems we already have so as to take the heat out of some, replace some with vastly improved environmental practices and thereby create a future which is calmer and oh so much more harmonious.

It is hereby suggested that there may be two main strands to bringing about this redirecting of the train thus (1) reforming and perhaps creating anew, reputable international bodies which can make provision for all the various strands of interdependent aims, including economic and current banking reform, to attain an agreed optimum ethos for mankind and (2) immediately initiating and boosting the green agenda in its many forms, starting with the initial creation of local horticultural initiatives, which serve to educate people, from the ground up, in the inherent value and purpose of sustainable harmony and balance with the natural world around us.

Bodies to effect aims of universal ethos

It might be suggested that there will be need for formation of a global international body with agreed peak standards in wholesome, upstanding, legally-binding statutes of economic, ecological, legal and humane principles, in accordance with an agreed ideal ethos. In relation to these statutes, there will be a scale of levels in achieving these standards which individual countries will need to aspire to, so as to attain according levels of responsibility, acumen and award, as an aid and example to those countries rising up the scale. These statutes will need to embody agreed levels of honourability, honesty, steadfastness, aim for excellence, and procedures for review and self-examination, so as to eradicate any possibility of corruption in those in positions of public administration and power.

Core aims to achieve

As a consequence of the pitfalls in western economic policy, evidenced by the world economic crash of 2008/9, a new economic strategy will need to evolve, on sustainable grounds.

Agriculture and Energy

A requirement may need to exist on all countries to put in place agri-economic plans for high levels of agricultural self-sufficiency. Countries will have different levels of capability on this level, and these differences can be accommodated by local agreements between countries for mutual trade to achieve required agricultural and food stocks. The idea is to agree a sustainable and renewable plan which can last for generations, perhaps forever, based on climate and geological facets. The reasons for this level of predictability in supply is central to what peoples currently require – namely a predictable supply of common foodstuffs easily obtainable.

It is suggested that local planning create networks of **local centres** for market-gardening of fruit/veg and horticultural items, perhaps in satellite formation, which will be mandatory around all centres of population from the smallest hamlets to largest cities. These centres may incorporate market activity, may also supply to local markets, as well as into the supermarket chain if desirable. These centres will be vital to the theory that much of what we need for sustainable living is largely free and renewable. By their proximity to populations they will also, vitally, nurture in mankind the sense of our primal connection with the earth, feed our innate sense of well-being at producing our own food and flora/fauna at negligible cost, as a basis for the rest of our lives and for passing on to the next generations. I imagine that such local centres could look like very attractive places indeed with, typically, fields around population centres turned into large areas for seasonal root vegetables, salad produce, small and large, flowers, plants and shrubs nurtured for adorning the local area, garden fruits such as raspberries, strawberries, blackcurrants, gooseberries, tomatoes, apples, plums, pears and whatever is local to that part of the world. With such beautiful produce available at negligible cost for production, other interesting activities would flourish, such as preservation, enhanced interest in culinary skills and mutual sharing of the attractive products of such enhanced usage.

It has been in the public awareness recently of a story which demonstrates such delectable success over such a scheme, where in one of the largest public housing estates in London, a school, which served the many disadvantaged youth of the locality, initiated schemes of horticulture from seed and soil to produce, which greatly engaged the young people, many of whom had growing-up problems, in such a productive way, that the exam pass rate soared from 4% to 100%. That is fact and that is the reality. The horticultural activity was then complemented by cookery schools, where often big teenage boys were seen to revel in learning the art of cuisine, from the produce that they had nurtured in the open air from and within nature. They spoke eloquently and convincingly about the sense of confidence which working with nature had engendered in them. This is proof positive that this strategy for people is full-proof and guaranteed.

From the economic subsistence perspective, these **local agricultural centres** will also be places where those who do not have any other employment, can find work or activity, perhaps for enhanced remuneration of their limited income/benefits, or on a voluntary basis. This could apply equally to those on limited employment, some ill/disabled and also pensioners who wish to keep active and continue to contribute to society and the economy. The possibilities for other aspects of local social renewal are also endless around such centres, and they must be run in accordance with established standards of practice on every level, effected by local governmental bodies. These centres may also be expanded to develop **local farming centres** for livestock and dairy with the added benefits of rural experience for those engaged with it.

The purpose of **local agricultural centres** is to foster a sense of sustainability and the value of reward from working with nature, to give mankind a connection with and a sense of our important and primal connection with nature and the produce of our food-stuffs for basic subsistence. But these local food production centres would also be complemented by the existing substantial food-supply chain and supermarket sector, with all the accordant food safety regulation and standards.

Energy

Regarding electricity production these will need to be based on methods which are as renewable as possible and/or as clean as possible. This could include nuclear, where properly administered, as it is a highly efficient, economic way of generating power. It is suggested that nuclear plants should only be only in remote and unfarmable areas, a safe distance from life, perhaps in desert areas where appropriate.

It is also a suggestion that there be a substantial reduction in long-distance travel, nationally and internationally, based largely around business ventures which support far-distant communities and nations to evolve their own society to agreed acceptable standards. Regarding emigration en masse it might be encouraged that peoples develop a better way of life in their own country and for their own people with all necessary support and incentive from the global international bodies established for this purpose.

Economic and Industrial

A vital component of this new way of living would be that, because each country is more self-sufficient in vital supplies, the amount of capital being interchanged at the higher echelons of the economy will be substantially reduced, thereby reducing the level of economic dependence between countries and international banking institutions and, critically, greatly reducing the concept of a country's debt.

Banks must be regulated so that a substantially higher level of capital will have to exist around lending, banks exist to lend on a more conservative and national level only, international lending will be effected by large organisations such as the IMF and World Bank, rather than by a network of international banks. A much larger % of corporate profits will go to such organisations as the IMF and World Bank, on something akin to a 'pawn-broking' service, where this Global Bank would be driven by statutes agreed under universal principles, to lend capital, and give aid where appropriate, to nations and organisations which are trying to rise along the scale of development to agreed international standards. This Global Bank would have sufficiently large capital so as to enable lending back to contributing corporations on a contributory scale basis and at minimum interest levels in accordance with level of contribution, to enable such corporates to continue efficient growth worldwide and so as to greatly encourage success, profit and entrepreneurialism. However the lending practices will also be based on strict rules on ethical practice of corporations, and also for micro and medium sized ventures where the aim is for the common good and their business plans realistic.

Because of the level of technological industrialisation already achieved in the 20th and 21st centuries, which mean that many traditional manual industrial jobs have been displaced by large scale automation and robots, it is a reality that there will not be enough work to gainfully occupy an ever-increasingly growing world population, therefore one consideration is to facilitate more women working in caring and domestic roles, perhaps not as conventional paid jobs but subsidised, by law, by partners and by benefits. As is the traditional role of man, they will all be expected to occupy paid jobs and, by law, a certain % of earnings would be allocated to spouses/partners, family and household bills. For those women with strong skills in any of the professions, their path through professional life will always be open and protected by strict equality laws. The main purpose of this plan is to take account of the serious situation of future unemployment because of high industrialisation and rapidly-expanding populations worldwide.

On the subject of male and female, there is no argument that we have typically different attributes as human beings, many of which are in common, but there are places where we each have our own strengths. Men's attributes tend to be more in the logical, practical and unemotional perspectives, whereby women's strengths tend to be in aspects of colour, form, connectedness, softness, caring and providing homestead comforts. On the intellectual front, there may not be any differences between what women and men attain. However, I believe that another highly desirable trait should be that there be a **greater presence of mature people, especially**

middle-aged men, in visibly apparent public roles in society. By this I mean in local and communal positions where they meet the public every day, such as running retail outlets, cafes, restaurants so that they are very much on the street. I believe it is a fundamental requirement of our human nature that all ages expect competent men to be visible and active in the local community, to give a sense of assuredness that everything is ok and to give back-bone and a feeling of security in the local environs. It is by this means that we can all feel a sense of home about our local community, a security to grow and achieve and a healthy respect for the strata of society. It is by this means that our young people can grow in a sense of security and respectful accountability. While men fulfil these roles of protection in our society, women can still excel in providing the soft home-coming qualities which all require to feel loved and safe in their own communities.

Cultural and Anthropological

It is a vital suggestion and outcome from consideration of our common needs, that we allow for the many and varied cultural origins of different peoples. I believe this to be a critical element of our realisation and we, especially in the west, must stop to recognise it now. Too much of our current world order is expected to revolve around modern materialistic culture. While there are many good outcomes of this mode, there is also a presumption that this is the only medium that mankind must grow along. We must take a step back, to recognise the many rich cultural, historical backgrounds and ways of life of all our nations throughout the world, and it is a vital component that we give credence and space for survival of these in every country, with the proviso that the emphasis be on attitudes of culture which are amicable to our neighbours rather than on offensive episodes in our history to others in the past. Thereby peoples may have pride in their historic origins and grow with pride and honour and mutual respect into the future.

We must surely recognise that this is the core of the attitude which we must take, not least because this is the very nature of the reasons why other countries have such vehement objection, stance and aggression, as much of the Arab world or North Korea towards the USA and the capitalist West in the present day.

It may seem to some that adoption of such statutes of common ethos, would become boring, unchallenging, and uncompetitive. On the contrary, the challenge is to each individual, to rid themselves of their partial views and possible dysfuntion, a task which may take some of us generations to effect. There will always be the healthy competition to effect a better, perfect practice of universal ethos, thereby demanding greater intellect, steadfastness, love, thrift, co-operation, honesty, accountability, responsibility and self-reliance and growth. But the greatest achievement will be that, each in our own cultures, will revolve around the graceful practices of our own culture, finding harbour each day in the comforts of domestic and communal life, basking in the abundance which nature provides around us and knowing when to quit when we are ahead.

The prize to attain - universal peace and contentment

Two-thirds of the world's peoples still do not have most of their primary needs met on a daily basis. This challenge will not allow much boredom for the foreseeable future. On the contrary, the accumulative effect of us becoming more aware of our roots in the best things in life being free in nature, recognition of our cultural heritage and what we can contribute and share of this with each other, taking time to imbibe this in our local areas, pride and self-respect and accountability in achieving the honourable statutes of our universal nature with each other, while making use of the many wonderful technological tools that we have at our disposal at this point in history, we stand to develop a model for the future which is sustainable, in recognition of nature, culture and in respect of other, and less ridden by competition, illusion of the need for frenetic incessant growth. Thereby we have means for a peaceful route through life where needs are met, no-one is jeopardised, where we maintain what is best in life and we have a structure whereby we can discuss and review our plans for the way forward for all peoples and for the future.

Spiritual fulfillment

Thus for those who believe in a spiritual destiny, we have a pathway to achieve what our God requires of us, which is to commit ourselves to live daily with joy and love and steadfast honour, in the ways of God and in service for our fellow man so that we all have a means to attain the happiness and peace that is our ultimate human and divine destiny.

Made in the USA
Charleston, SC
05 February 2014